C000298832

Rachel Turner has been a full-time c[...]
the UK and the National Children'[...]
She continues to consult, speak at c[...]
parents, children and youth workers around the UK and Europe. Her
work has brought her into contact with thousands of children and families
through mainstream New Wine summer events, parish weekends, schools,
and daily encounters in her own church. Rachel's first book 'Parenting
Children for a Life of Faith was published by BRF in 2010. Visit www.
rachelturner.org.uk to find out more about Rachel and her ministry.

Text copyright © Rachel Turner 2014
The author asserts the moral right
to be identified as the author of this work

Published by
The Bible Reading Fellowship
15 The Chambers, Vineyard
Abingdon, OX14 3FE
United Kingdom
Tel: +44 (0)1865 319700
Email: enquiries@brf.org.uk
Website: www.brf.org.uk
BRF is a Registered Charity

ISBN 978 0 85746 163 6

First published 2014
10 9 8 7 6 5 4 3 2 1 0
All rights reserved

Acknowledgments
Unless otherwise stated, scripture quotations are taken from The Holy Bible, New International
Version (Anglicised edition) copyright © 1973, 1978, 1984, 2011 by Biblica (formerly
International Bible Society). Used by permission of Hodder & Stoughton Publishers, a
Hachette UK company. All rights reserved. 'NIV' is a registered trade mark of Biblica (formerly
International Bible Society). UK trademark number 1448790.

Scripture quotations marked NCV are taken from the New Century Version®, copyright ©
2005 by Thomas Nelson, Inc. Used by permission. All rights reserved.

Scripture quotations marked CEV are taken from the Contemporary English Version of the
Bible, published by HarperCollins Publishers, copyright © 1991, 1992, 1995 American Bible
Society.

Cover photo: © Bounce/Getty Images

Every effort has been made to trace and contact copyright owners for material used in this
resource. We apologise for any inadvertent omissions or errors, and would ask those concerned
to contact us so that full acknowledgment can be made in the future.

A catalogue record for this book is available from the British Library

Printed and bound by CPI Group (UK) Ltd, Croydon CR0 4YY

Parenting children

for a life of purpose

Empowering children to become who they are called to be

Rachel Turner

For my son Caleb. I am so grateful that you are mine.

Acknowledgments

The Sanctuary Centre for Justice and Worship, thank you for generously allowing our joint work on the six-article series exploring Worship and Justice at Every Age to be the launching point for several of the chapters in this book.

Liz Baddaley and Jill Andrews, thank you for your friendship, encouragement, and determined love. You constantly reveal more of God's character to me, and you inspire me to be the best I can be.

Caleb Turner, thank you for being so patient with me every time I had to type instead of play. You make my heart sing.

Mark Turner, thank you, my stalwart husband, for carving space for me when I didn't see any, forcing encouragement on me when I was refusing hope, and for daily believing that this book was important and possible.

My mother, Susan Hart, thank you for reading more versions of this book than anyone ever should, and for sharing with me your wisdom, skill and honesty to help me shape it.

My dad, Terry Hart, thank you for letting me steal Mom for weeks on end, and for making me laugh and get distracted when I desperately needed it.

My church, Harrogate New Life Church, thank you for giving me the freedom and grace to let me disappear to write, and for your willingness to go on a blind journey with me.

Thank you to all my friends who encouraged me and supported our family while I wrote: Elaine Webster, Elle Bird, Fiona East, Cathy Burwell, David and Brittney Withers, James and Susie Yeates, and more.

Contents

Foreword 7

Introduction 9

Chapter 1: Identity, relationship and purpose 13

Chapter 2: Telling the whole story 19

Chapter 3: Positioning for empowerment 29

Chapter 4: Foundational purpose 39

Chapter 5: Seeing power in the mirror 43

Chapter 6: Learning the way of love 59

Chapter 7: Finding our calling 75

Chapter 8: Shaping our response 85

Chapter 9: Poised to act 99

Chapter 10: Part of the body 111

Chapter 11: FAQs 123

Appendix A: Sharing the vision with your leadership team
and congregation 133

Appendix B: Models for implementation 137

*

Foreword

This book fills me with hope. Its author believes that children are powerful individuals who can have a profound effect for God—now as well as in the future. She champions the truth that we were created for something much bigger than merely living our own lives or achieving our own dreams, and that partnering with God to be a world-changer has no biblically recognised minimum age limit.

Like its prequel, *Parenting Children for a Life of Faith* (BRF, 2010), the book combines clear, visionary thinking with solid biblical grounding. It voices a passionate realism that recognises both the urgency and achievability of the transformation it longs for. The real-life stories demonstrate the author's deep awareness of the competing pressures facing young people, and the practical ideas model the way change comes simply by allowing new thinking to enter existing discipleship approaches.

Our churches and our world desperately need the kind of children and adults that *Parenting Children for a Life of Purpose* invites us to be. We are called first and foremost to respond to our Father's love by living out Jesus' command to love God and others with every fibre of our beings (Luke 10:27) and by making him known to the ends of the earth (Matthew 28:16–20).

In an age of me-centred thinking and celebrity culture, I am deeply encouraged to find a book on calling that doesn't start from a place of ascertaining individuals' specific gifts or strengths. Instead, it asks us to be inspired by Christ and his call to the whole church, and to make this our primary purpose. As we live this out with our resources, talents and time, we will discover that everything we do is invested with new meaning.

Our purpose is really to ask the same question again and again in every situation we face, from personal relational issues through to globally powerful consumer choices, campaigns or career paths:

'Jesus, what could I do here to put you and your other children before myself?'

Imagine if this kind of thinking were to inspire a generation! My prayer is that it will.

Liz Baddaley
Author, worship leader and co-founder of the Sanctuary

*

Introduction

'OK, so here's the thing,' he began, rubbing his short greying hair with one hand as he quickly scanned the other picnic tables filled with families laughing. He paused as he tried to figure out a way to begin. 'My daughter is eight. She is tiny, just a child. I look at her and see my baby, my precious little daughter. She comes home and tells me that her heart beats fast and happy when she thinks about helping people get close to God. She wants to start talking to people about God, now. In church and out of church. She feels like this is what she is meant to do. If she said this when she was a teenager, I would understand better. But talk me through how my little, tiny child is going to do this in her everyday life, and what I am supposed to do? Is this OK? How do I help? How do I ground her and give her a foundation? She's just eight!'

Most of us would agree that our children have specialness inside them. We can see possibilities of the future flicker in their hearts and souls as they grow. We look forward to cheering them on as they get older and 'discover' their calling in life. But what if there is more for them now? What if the flickers we see are meant for use in their everyday life as well as the future?

We all hear of extraordinary children doing extraordinary things. We see them on the news or in magazines. Billy saw a need and did a fundraiser and now has funded over 600 wells in Africa. 'Good for him,' we discount as we make lunches in the morning. 'How much effort did his mum have to put into that?' Gemma organised a postcard campaign to the prime minister to discuss child poverty. Over 100,000 postcards were sent. 'Weird political child,' we judge as we drive around. 'No way would a real child want to do that.' Those big stories can seem to us to exist for those families who have extra time to do it, or for the unique child who cares about issues like that, far removed from our one-year-old mashing bananas into the carpet or our seven-year-old boy who adores football or our teen girl whose phone is attached to her hand. 'Raising children with purpose,' we think, 'takes effort, time... and someone else's children.' Or does it?

Children are designed to be purposeful, to have power within themselves and with the Spirit, and to live life heart-to-heart and in step with the Father. We often mistakenly think that 'purpose' is the same as 'accomplishments', and we can become overwhelmed with the thought of facilitating such achievements in our children. But that isn't what true spiritual purpose is.

Having purpose is to exist for a reason, to live and sacrifice for something bigger than ourselves, and to pursue the will of God in our lives and in the world. Whether or not our children's purpose will result in being in leadership, I don't know. Leadership is just one result of purpose, not the inevitable conclusion. Purpose is expressed by faithfully choosing to walk each day in relationship with God, knowing that we are a part of his plans today, tomorrow, and the next day. Our children deserve to have a life filled with purpose.

This book isn't '354 Things to Add to Your Week to Raise Purposeful Children', because to be honest I can't cram anything else into my life, and I assume you are the same. This book is about allowing our children their spiritual birthright to be purposeful and powerful. It is about training our eyes to see beyond what we hope and want for them, in order to see who God is shaping them to be now and what he is calling them to do here. It is about easily and lightly coaching our children to live 'heart-connected' with the Lord and to walk in their purpose every day to affect their home, community, church and nation.

This book is my offering to you, to encourage you and equip you to raise your children to be who God has made them to be, so that they can walk in close relationship with God, doing all God has for them to do today, tomorrow, the next day and for all eternity. I believe that this is a key part of our ordinary calling as parents, and that God designed it to be light and joy-filled. May God bless you mightily, give you lots of sleep, and help you to see clearly the joy and the fruit of parenting your children for a life of purpose.

*

— Chapter 1 —

Identity, relationship and purpose

Her eyes were glowing as she beamed a smile at me. For the past 15 minutes, nine-year-old Jessi had been sitting on the ground, praying for an adult who had come to the side of the room during a church service to meet with God. She had confidently and gently prayed for this woman, handed her tissues when she cried, and throughout the 15 minutes whispered encouragements and prayers to her as she helped the older woman meet with God. As the grateful woman went back to her seat, I leaned over to check in on Jessi. 'How was that?' I asked. She could barely contain herself. 'It's amazing. I'm normally really shy and can't say what I want to, but when it's God's words I feel strong and all the words that are in my heart actually come out of my mouth.' I asked if she wanted to continue to pray with people and she nodded emphatically. 'I want to do it all the time! Because I think this is what I'm meant to do. I think he made me this way, to do this—help people who hurt meet with God. I'm me when I do it. I want to do it loads.'

Purpose strikes to the core of us as humans. The search for purpose is everywhere. Why am I here? What is life all about? Who am I supposed to be? What am I supposed to do with my life? The questions resonate for all of us.

The truth is that our children are powerful people called to a great purpose on this earth. And we as parents can help them find it and live it each day.

When we begin to think about how to parent children for a life of purpose, I find that it's most helpful to look at how we were created and what we were created for. For that, we go to our Father: the first parent, the ultimate parent.

Genesis 1 and 2 tell us the story of the creation of people. God was in the process of creating the world and he had the idea to make people: children for himself. He carefully and lovingly made them in his likeness, and then he spoke to them. 'So God created humans to be like himself; he made men and women. God gave them his blessing and said...' (Genesis 1:27–28, CEV).

We assume that God's initial doting was similar to ours. When we first meet our children, we often want just to hold them and watch them. We tell them how beautiful they are, and we want to protect them forever. But look at what God does with his new children. He blesses them, which I'm sure was lovely, and then says to them, 'Have a lot of children! Fill the earth with people and bring it under your control. Rule over the fish in the ocean, the birds in the sky, and every animal on the earth' (v. 28).

His children are brand new, and the first thing he does is give them a job! They are fresh out of the package, and yet they have been given a purpose for now and a vision for how to develop that in the future. God considered it vital to impart to his newly formed children their purpose.

Identity, relationship and purpose in the Bible

Adam and Eve were created in God's image, directly able to see and experience their own similarities to him. They knew who they were and what their identity was: they were created by the Creator, and were his children.

They were also given a relationship—a relationship with God as his children, able to hear his voice, interact with him and know him. If you look at Genesis 2 and 3, you will see that Adam and Eve conversed with God and knew his voice well. They even knew the familiar sound of him walking in the garden. They had a natural and real connection to God.

And almost immediately, they were given purpose: a task, a vision, a thing to give themselves to. All three are important in their own right but are also inextricably linked. God gave them their identity and lived in relationship with them, and that experience shaped how they found and walked in their purpose.

We can see this pattern throughout scripture. The people we most admire tend to have identity, relationship and purpose emblazoned in their spirits.

Abram's *identity* was shaped as God told him who he was and would be: a blessing to nations, the father of many nations, and fruitful. God even changed Abram's name to reflect the new identity he was shaping in him, from Abram (which means father) to Abraham (father of many). God drew him into a covenant, a formal binding *relationship*, and talked with him openly and often, in direct conversation with him throughout his life. God gave Abraham a mighty *purpose*, and he obeyed faithfully (and sometimes not) as he pursued his purpose in response to God's direction and in confidence of who God made him to be. Abraham lived his purpose walking the length and breadth of the land he was given, interceding for people, and holding firm to the tangible promises of God (see Genesis 12, 13 and 17).

Jeremiah was only a child when God told him that before he formed him in his mother's womb, he had appointed Jeremiah as a prophet to the nations. His *identity* as a prophet had been planned even before he was created. God added to his identity, saying that he also made him as a fortified city, an iron pillar and a bronze wall to stand against the whole land. God promised his constant voice in *relationship*, his presence and his faithfulness to rescue Jeremiah. God also laid out clearly Jeremiah's *purpose*: to go boldly and without fear, speaking the words he would give him to kings, priests and people in order to change the nations. Without his purpose, Jeremiah wouldn't have his identity. Without the tangible relationship with God, he would have nothing to speak and no purpose to fulfil (see Jeremiah 1).

In the life of Jesus we see the intertwining of the three. When Jesus was baptised, God spoke and named Jesus as his Son, affirming his *identity*. Jesus walked confident in this every day, accomplishing all his Father had for him to do because of his unique identity. He lived life in *relationship* with the Father and the Holy Spirit, ministering with the Spirit and often spending time on his own in prayer to the Father. His *purpose* on earth was clear: to redeem us to the Father and to show us how to walk in relationship with him. Identity, relationship and purpose are expressed best in Jesus showing us the perfect balance of how to live healthily with all three (see the Gospels, for example Matthew 3:17; 9:13; Luke 4:16–21; John 3:16–17; 17:1–26).

The examples can go on and on: Moses, Joshua, Gideon, David, Peter, Mary and Paul. Identity, relationship and purpose gave people strength and ability to live great and significant lives.

An entwined approach

This entwined and balanced approach is something we naturally do as parents. As our children grow, we deliberately help them to understand themselves and their place in our family (*identity*). We help them to feel secure in their relationship with us and assist them in navigating their relationships with others (*relationship*). We also give them the skills and understanding to be productive, conscientious and independent members of society (*purpose*). We do it so naturally that we often don't notice how holistic our approach really is.

When it comes to growing our children spiritually, though, we can often lose confidence in our holistic approach. We can lean towards focusing heavily on identity and relationship. Our instinct can be to want our children to know that they are loved by us and by God and be comfortable in that. But when we begin to face spiritual purpose we can shy away, leaving it out almost entirely for the first decade of our children's lives, not wanting to drop the bombshell that there are other requirements that we have to 'do' as part of the Christian deal. We don't want to stress them out or make them feel pressured to perform, so we often leave purpose on the sideline, to be picked up at a later time when it is convenient. In doing this, I believe we are stunting the spiritual growth and happiness of our children.

Without purpose, children's faith can become insular and selfish, focusing on their experiences first. Boredom and confusion can creep into their faith because it has become purely about what they are getting out of it.

Without purpose, children are robbed of the power of their God-given identity. What is the use of having authority in Christ, if you have nowhere to use it? What is the use of being unique, if you cannot apply it to something?

Without purpose, children's relationships with God will be limited. God is a God of action and creation, as well as of love. He has purposes and plans. He is in the world accomplishing and doing. Purpose reveals a different side of God, adding depth to our understanding of God's heart in action. It is important for our children to know the fullness of God, which includes his purposes and actions, so that they can learn to see him in the world and choose to join him in his plans.

God is a God of completeness. When identity, relationship and purpose exist side by side, our children can walk in spiritual health, thriving confidently in their relationship with God, and in being an essential part of something bigger than themselves. We cannot and should not teach one without the others.

What we will do in this book

Given that an entwined approach to spiritual growth is important, why a book specifically on purpose? In essence, this book is a continuation of what was begun in my first book, *Parenting Children for a Life of Faith: Helping children meet and know God* (BRF, 2010). I believe it is crucial that a child is God-connected, not just God-smart, and *Parenting Children for a Life of Faith* exists to empower parents to feel confident in spiritually growing children to thrive in a two-way heart-to-heart relationship with God. Purpose is a natural expression of our relationship with God, and so this book on purpose cannot exist in isolation from the ideas in my first book.

This book seeks to explore in depth how to grow children spiritually to know and live out their God-given purpose. It will give you ideas on how to help them entwine their purpose with their identity and relationship with God and others, and how to disciple them daily in being powerful people in this world.

*

— Chapter 2 —

Telling the whole story

Eleven-year-old Hannah scrunched her face at me. 'I'm not sure I even want to be a Christian anymore. It's so boring. Do this. Do that. Make God happy. And it doesn't make any sense. If God was real and actually here, why did the tsunami happen? If he loves everybody so much, then why doesn't he help?'

Over and over again, I have run across parents whose children struggle with the same questions. Children look at the world and see so much that confuses them when they try to match up what they see to their faith. They can't see God's purposes, nor can they find their own purpose within them.

We can be faced with this barrage of questions on a daily basis. Our own life circumstances and difficult stories about our friends, our communities and our nation often swirl around in our thoughts. These stories swirl around in our children's minds, too. We are desperate for our children to have an anchor that will help them to weather these storms in life—and not just to weather them: to flourish in them.

An incomplete foundation

All of us want the best for our children's faith, whether our children are one or eight or 14 or 35 years old. In our efforts to help our children connect with God and acquire faith, we often shelter them from the whole story, the complete story of the gospel. By giving them only an incomplete understanding of the gospel story, we actually disconnect them from God, who would be their anchor and who wants to hold them firmly and empower them with faith and purpose through the storms of life.

The problem is that sometimes we find it difficult to break down the whole gospel story—and so we end up leaving out key elements rather than trying to find ways to translate them into simpler concepts. We decide that we will add them in later, but we rarely do. It sounds harmless enough, but the results are significant: many children grow up in the church with only a partial understanding of the gospel story, with an incomplete foundation.

It can sometimes look like the diagram on the next page.

Example of the widening narrative

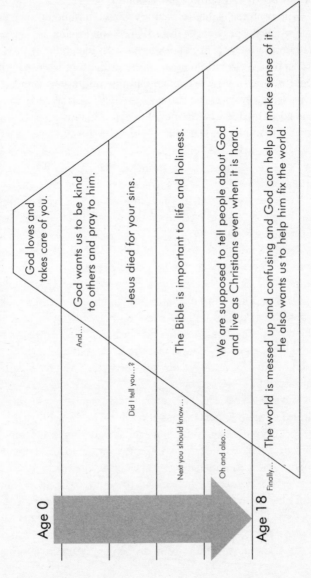

God loves and takes care of you.

And... God wants us to be kind to others and pray to him.

Did I tell you...? Jesus died for your sins.

Next you should know... The Bible is important to life and holiness.

Oh and also... We are supposed to tell people about God and live as Christians even when it is hard.

Finally... The world is messed up and confusing and God can help us make sense of it. He also wants us to help him fix the world.

Age 0

Age 18

21

When we first begin to talk to our children about God, we often start by telling them that they are loved, welcomed and precious to their Father. We really want them to bed down in that safeness. Then we add a bit of the story: because we are loved, we should try to please God. After a couple of years of space, we gently slide the gospel in, trying to explain salvation and Jesus' sacrifice lightly. We add the 'shoulds' of being a Christian, with spiritual disciplines and lists of what God requires. We let that bed down for a while. And then once they start looking bored, we talk about holiness and evangelism and mission and try to excite them about the obligation of 'spreading the gospel'. Eventually, as our children approach adulthood, we feel safe to suggest that maybe they may want to get involved with doing something about the hurt in the world and begin to discuss the more grey areas of being in the world as a Christian.

By the end of this journey of childhood, the initial message—love, safety and unconditional approval—has turned into something totally different. It is now about behaviour obligations and restrictions, responsibilities, ritual, tradition, and a pressure to 'share' with others and do something about the broken world if they want. And being loved, and occasionally safe. Meanwhile, the world is happening around them and to them and they don't have a framework for understanding it, their place in it, or where God is and what he is doing about it.

If we want our children to be able to stand firm in this life and find their place, then we need to tell them the whole story of the gospel from the beginning. If we tell it well, then everything can be tied to it. The whole story will provide a theological framework for them to grow in understanding of God and the world. It will provide a story big enough to live in and to be a part of. It will provide a story in which all things can be understood and next steps can be known. Telling the whole story is important. As they get older, the story of the gospel will deepen, but not change. There will never be a surprise that leaps out, just a deepening of understanding.

We instinctively know how to do this. No matter what the story, it can be told simply in six sentences in a baby's board book or it can be expanded into an entire three-hour movie! The story is the same, but the depth of understanding and detail grows with the telling.

So what is the whole gospel and how does it relate to reality?

At every age, we can translate the gospel story into language and concepts that children can begin to understand. I find using the following six points, which are inspired by the structure and content of John 3:16, a helpful way to make sure I am telling the whole story:

1. God is love. He made all things from his vast creativity and love. He created man and woman to be loved by him and to respond to that love, and, in turn, they are to love all those around them. God loves and fully knows each individual—us, and everyone else.
2. People walked away from God. The world and its people chose, and keep choosing, to separate themselves from God. Instead of loving him and loving other people, we choose to love ourselves, to love our stuff, to love getting our way, and to love only the people who give us what we want.

   This makes us move further away from God and further towards evil. Even people who try to love God and other people do this sometimes. It isn't good for us or for other people. It affects decisions and the very way we build society, because if people in power act this way, it has even more impact. It creates lots of bad consequences in the world: people in pain, people not having enough to eat, people being treated badly just because of where they live or what they look like, people being isolated, or people trying to fix problems with things that don't work and simply make them sadder or more selfish.

This separation between the world's way and God's way is so big that some people don't even believe God exists anymore, especially when they look at the mess we have all made.

3. Jesus cleared a way back to closeness with God. Living in a broken world can be hard, but we don't need to be afraid or give up hope, because God is bigger than all of this. Through Jesus, and through what he did for us when he died and rose again, we have a way back to love and the relationships with God and other people that he intended at the start.

4. God is active in the world and we can partner with him to transform it. Knowing God and being his friends means that we can love him. We can be forgiven for all the clutter that gets into our hearts and can love other people again properly. If we follow him, he invites us to work with him to help ourselves, other people and the whole world to move away from evil to good. That means working with him to share his story with others, to stand up for what is fair, to care for the poor and hurting, to pray for others, to be generous; and much, much more.

5. He gives us his power through his Holy Spirit to join with him in putting love at the centre of everything again. All that is broken in the world is being changed. None of it is as big as God or beyond being changed by his love as we join in with that work. No one has gone so far that he or she can't come to know God again.

6. One day, it will all be the way God meant it to be forever. One day, when Jesus comes again, the whole world will be completely good and loving again, and there will never be anything else that gets in the way of us loving God and each other.

This is the whole story. It's still not the full story—there is a lot of depth still to come—but there are no surprises left for later. There is also a clear sense of humanity's purpose: to love God, to live in community, to experience the abundant life Christians are called to in loving God, and to work with him to change themselves and the world.

There will be better ways to summarise, translate and explain the whole story for different ages, backgrounds and personalities, but it's important to ensure that none of these core elements is missing. When the scriptural story is the core, our experiences and reading of scripture and theology can be tied to it, so that nothing exists in isolation from the adventure story of God. Instead of the triangle model of a widening story given to children and teens as they grow, they can have a consistent simple model with the core story always at the centre. As children and teens grow, more knowledge and experiences can be tied to the core story that deepens as the child gets older.

For instance, a four-year-old will know the core story and will have a few theological points and life experiences to tie to it.

By the time the child is ten, the story stays the same, but the child is able to tie to it more and more of his knowledge and experiences of God and life. See the diagram overleaf.

Orienting to the story

This core story approach means that our purpose and our actions can be easily linked in to the identity, relationship and calling we have within the whole story. When we talk with our children about the importance of generosity and sharing, the reason is not just because God wants us to do so. It's because God loves other people as much as he loves us, and other people have needs and wants and are hurting. When we are willing to love God and other people more than we love our belongings, we can partner with God to lift others up and help minister to those more in need by giving them what we have, happily and freely.

When we look at the news and see the horror of what is happening, we don't have to be confused by the 'why?' questions.

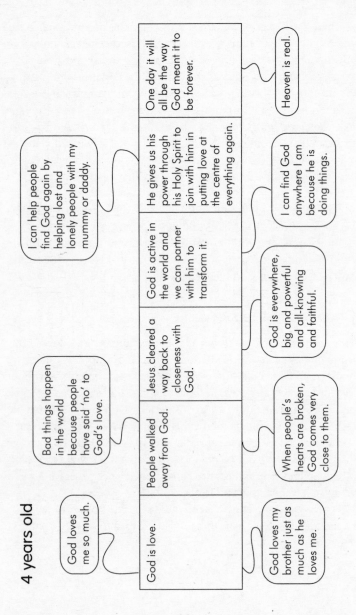

4 years old

10 years old

God's love isn't dependent on what we do or don't do.

Loving people so well that everyone is amazed is one of the most powerful tools we have.

The world is broken because people choosing themselves over God and others created a mess.

There is nothing in this world that can't be redeemed and restored by God – hope always exists.

When a natural disaster happens, God is already there speaking to people, intervening, rescuing, loving, and comforting.

This will not go on forever; there is a plan beyond here and now!

Jesus is our Saviour, restoring us to God and taking the consequences for our sins.

I need transformation as much as everyone else and the Holy Spirit will walk with me, speak to me, and work in me.

One day it will all be the way God meant it to be forever.

God is love.

People walked away from God.

Jesus cleared a way back to closeness with God.

God is active in the world and we can partner with him to transform it.

He gives us his power through his Holy Spirit to join with him in putting love at the centre of everything again.

I can do my bit to pray for the restoration that God will bring.

The design of God was that no one would ever be lost or lonely, or would ever doubt their lovability.

We can read in the Bible how God feels about the mess and evil that exists and why it happens over and over.

When people do bad things, God didn't make them; it was their choice to choose the wrong and broken way.

God is everywhere, big and powerful and all-knowing and faithful.

When my mum yells at me and it feels like I have absolutely nothing left in me to love her back, I can sit in God's love to recharge.

I am called to be a purposeful person seeking the lost, hurt, enslaved, broken and lonely.

Jesus commanded us to go to all nations, preaching the gospel, healing the sick, raising the dead, and casting out demons to wow them with his love and to break the power of the enemy.

The bully at school has some need in them, or some broken bit that God can heal.

We can say, 'I'm reminded of that verse in the Bible when Jesus says, "In this world you will have trouble. But take heart! I have overcome the world" (John 16:33). This world is so full of awful trouble, isn't it? My heart just wants to pray for those people right now. God, thank you that you have overcome this world, and those people need you. Please rescue them, and send your angels to protect them and comfort them. Create safe places for them. Help them, God.' We can then empower our children to connect with God, heart-to-heart, about their feelings.

We can highlight how life scenarios fit into the whole story and what that means for us and the people involved. In the case of a natural disaster, we could assure our children: 'God didn't send this tsunami. Earthquakes are a natural part of how the world works, and horrifically the consequences for people living in the impact zone are huge. But God is always at work being who he is: the rescuer, redeemer, comforter, protector. Can you see where God is and what he is doing in the midst of the mess? How can we help? What can we do?'

When our children know the whole story, they can find every experience in life in the story, and they can be empowered in their place within it.

*

— Chapter 3 —

Positioning for empowerment

It doesn't happen so much now in the Western world, but in the olden days, children's destinies were determined when they were small. A child of a cobbler more than likely would be a cobbler. The son of a farmer would be a farmer. The daughter of a king would be a princess or a queen. Some families' plans for their children were defined by birth order: the first would take over the business, the second would join the military, the third the clergy, and so on. For most children, even from before they were born, parents had a vision and a destiny. From the cradle they were given skills and values, as training for their future. Toys would reflect what they would grow up to do, and they would be given chores and training in the specialism of their destiny. Their time with their parents blended with equipping for their future. In some scenarios, they would be apprenticed to another family to learn a trade at seven or eleven or 14. From birth, children were treated as if they had a destiny that mattered.

Time has moved on, and most of us no longer decide for our children what we want them to do as a career. Most of us want our children to grow up to have a good, fulfilling job or calling, but we are often flexible about the particulars.

In the freedom that we now value for their future, we can miss the lifelong proactive training for their destiny from which previous generations have benefited. We no longer look at a three-year-old and instinctively think, 'What skills and values do I need to input into this child right now for him to live his future well?' It is important for us to remember that while we are not proactively growing our children for a specific, inevitable job, we still have a specific spiritual destiny in mind.

We want them to be children of God, friends of Christ, and ministers of the gospel through the power of the Spirit. We want them to be purposeful partners of the living God. That requires lifelong training, not an NVQ later in life.

Growing a foundation for children sets them on a lifelong path. In Proverbs 22:6 we read, 'Start children off on the way they should go, and even when they are old they will not turn from it.' Their spiritual purpose must begin from childhood, so that they not only experience a fullness of life now but also know how to grasp and live their purpose as adults.

God laid out his method of faith and purpose development for children, rooting it firmly in the ordinary life of family: 'Love the Lord your God with all your heart and with all your soul and with all your strength. These commandments that I give you today are to be on your hearts. Impress them on your children. Talk about them when you sit at home and when you walk along the road, when you lie down and when you get up. Tie them as symbols on your hands and bind them on your foreheads. Write them on the doorframes of your houses and on your gates' (Deuteronomy 6:5–9).

Family life is the beginning of destiny training. Family was designed that way. We as parents are perfectly placed to empower our children.

How do we do this?

The six-stage circle

We as parents hold such influence in our children's lives. It can be quite humbling when we think about the power we have in shaping another human being emotionally, physically, mentally and spiritually. We are put here for a reason—not just to care for a growing person, but to lay a foundation in them that will last a lifetime.

Your children are watching and learning about your identity, relationship and purpose from you—whether you are intentional about it or not. God placed you as a parent in your children's lives so that you could display to them what a real, authentic everyday life journey with him looks like. As you show your children what it looks like in you and others, you can coach them in their journey, empowering them to engage with God on their own.

As I have parented and worked in churches as a children's minister or youth worker, I have noticed that the most effective way of discipling a child in any scenario, for any value, is to take them on a journey, lightly but deliberately. I find it useful to see this discipleship as a circle, one stage leading to another. You will probably be able to recognise aspects of your parenting style within it and you may see some areas you are missing.

This journey is shown in the diagram below.

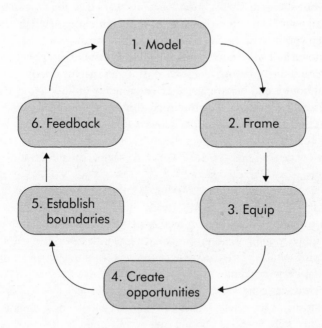

Here's an example of how it works:

I have a friend who loves Leeds United. His children love Leeds United. He didn't have to convince them about the merits of the football club or worry that they wouldn't like Leeds United when they grew up. He didn't restrain himself from trying to influence his children in terms of their football choice until they were 'old enough to choose for themselves'. Completely unconsciously, he discipled his children into a love of Leeds United, using this circle.

He modelled what living a life loving this football club meant. He couldn't not! He watched the matches on television, wore the T-shirts, defended his team vigorously to others in front of his children, cheered when they won, was gutted when they lost, and knew all the details of all the players and told his children all about them.

He sat his children down and framed for them how the game was played, how the coach was strategising, and why he loved this particular club so much. He framed for them why he attended the matches, and who he went with, and where they sat and why.

Since his children were tiny, he equipped them to love the team. He covered them in Leeds United kit: onesies and hats, scarves and pennants. He played football with them outside, and he chose to 'be' a certain player when playing. He bought them posters and taught them all they needed to know to be able to talk about player transfers and offside injustices.

He created opportunities for his children to experience the team, watching matches on television with them, and even letting them stay up late to watch the big matches. The momentous day arrived when he took his children to see the team play live in the stadium. Eventually, as they grew, these outings became a key part of their father–child bonding times.

This father light-heartedly established boundaries, swearing off the flying of any other colours in the house and jokingly ribbing his friends who supported another team. His children knew who he wanted them to support, make no mistake.

He gave his children fantastic feedback by roaring with laughter when they voiced an opinion in line with his own. He swept them up in a hug when they were indignant about a referee call. He listened to their questions carefully and answered with focus and passion.

Whether it's football, love of musicals or how to clean the house, this circle is often present in our parenting. When we harness this natural process deliberately to disciple our children spiritually, it can be a powerful tool.

You see, we were placed in our children's lives to do this easily. Each of these stages is a natural part of our lives with our children. We naturally *live life* in front of our children, *talk to them* about what is happening, *equip them* to do things for themselves, *create opportunities* for them to try things out, *establish boundaries* for them to live within and *chat to them* about how their behaviour impacts others.

Any value we want to instil in our children can be worked around this basic progress circle. I have come to disciple children in this way now almost unconsciously. Anything I want them to begin to own as a core value or belief, I simply choose to 'take it around the circle'. It doesn't require a lot of time or effort, just a choice.

To see this in action, let's take a value, a simple one you want your children to know in the depths of themselves. Let's use this example: 'Words always make an impact.'

Model

The first step is deliberately to create windows into your own life, so that your children can look in and see this value in action. We, as parents, have been designed and placed in our children's lives for many reasons. One of those reasons is to show the nitty-gritty reality of a life lived with God. Modelling is simply living life with God *while your children can see*, so that they can have glimpses into the inner workings of how to have a relationship of their own with

God, and how to live their purpose well. In this case, how do words affect you, and how do you use your words to affect others? You can model this by:

- consciously allowing your children to overhear you encouraging a friend or your partner
- putting up cards or letters that people have sent you to show how you value their words
- letting your children hear you saying, 'Just a second, before we leave I want to ask Bob about his surgery. Just asking makes him feel less lonely and it's so important to reach out to him.'

Frame

Framing is a way to teach our children how to see the world, so that they know how to respond. A picture frame highlights what is in it. It shows the boundaries of the picture and captures a moment in time to remember. It is essential that we create verbal picture frames around many things children see in their lives, especially when we want to train them in a skill or a value. Often we assume that children understand our motivations or actions, or the situation they are in, and we miss the opportunity to frame the situation for them. Take a moment to say, 'When you see this right here, this is what is happening spiritually. This is what God is doing. This is what is happening in my heart or in their hearts.' With our example of training children about the power of words:

- Let them into secrets of how others' communications have helped you. 'You know I was feeling really stressed today, but then I talked to Jill and she reminded me of all the positives of the situation. Her words really helped me calm down.' 'I so loved the sermon today. Sometimes just hearing about God totally challenges my mind.'
- Tell stories of how other people's name-calling or lies impacted

how you saw yourself or how you acted. 'Hearing you fight reminds of me of a time when I was your brother's age and my friend told me I was annoying. It punched me in the gut so much, and even to this day I sometimes get worried about being annoying. Isn't that amazing that his words hurt me so much that I sometimes still feel bad about it now? Pretty scary that a little thing like that can cause so much damage, isn't it?'

- Watch your children's favourite television programme with them and chat about the impact that words have on the characters.

Equip

Even after our children see the value in our lives physically and spiritually, and understand what it means and how to respond, they still need to be equipped to participate in it. Equipping children to experience success for themselves enables them to feel confident to take the next step. So what are some ways to equip them to appreciate and use words well?

Show them how words can be used in different ways, like tools; for instance, like a balm or cream: to soothe someone or something that is upset. Point out how your friend's words helped to soothe you, or how your children have used their words like a balm in the past. Brainstorm ideas of what could soothe someone when they are upset or irritated. Here's how I would describe other word tools for children to use:

- Blow dryer: when people are feeling all wet and crying and cold and lonely, some encouragement can warm them up and dry them off. What kind of words warm someone?
- Shield: when someone is being attacked or teased, our words can protect and shield them. If someone is making fun of you or a friend, what could you say to make it stop or to distract them?
- Sword: sometimes people believe things that are untrue about themselves or others; we can use our words to cut off lies from

people. Let's practise! I'll say something about me that is a lie, and you try using your words to help me know the truth. 'I'm rubbish all the time!' or 'He's stupid.' What would you say?

- Wisdom: sometimes people need your advice and opinion to help them to make decisions or to add something new and helpful to a group decision. In this family we want to hear your thoughts when we discuss things!
- Love and connection: when people are lonely or want to love and be loved, they need people to talk with them and listen to them. They need people with whom to share stories and memories and jokes. Have you ever felt left out? What did you wish people had done to help you feel connected? Where can you use your words to help other people feel loved and connected?

Talk about how God's words are powerful, and share how his words have affected your life and your family. Maybe put some on the walls, on the fridge or in baskets. As you go about your life, share how God's words soothe you or protect you or show you the truth and cut off a lie. Talk about how his wisdom and daily communication help to guide you and make you feel close to him.

Create opportunities

As parents, we can lay out a variety of opportunities for our children to practise what they are learning and to experience the joy—and wobbliness—of doing it themselves. When we create opportunities for them, we are defining a safe place for them to practise and fail, or try and succeed, where we can catch them and help them to process their experience. It is very important that our children fail around us, so that we can help them process those feelings and disciple them through all areas of purpose, not just easy or successful ones. Here are some ideas for creating opportunities to learn the power of words:

- Point out a person in church who is looking lonely and in need of some encouragement, and ask your children if they'd like to help with their words.
- Allow your children to input into your life and the lives of your family. Say, 'Johnny, your little brother is upset and could use some soothing words. Could you help?' Or, 'Your dad is feeling sad because he didn't get the new job. What could we say to make him feel encouraged?' Or, 'What do you think we should have for dinner?'

Establish boundaries

It is so helpful for children to know the boundaries of where their influence and responsibility ends, what behaviour is acceptable and what isn't, and where they can exercise their calling and where is not safe. Boundaries also help children to understand that they have power with which they need to be responsible, and that what they do matters.

Tell your children that, because words are so powerful, there need to be some boundaries to keep people safe. Whatever your lines are for what is acceptable or not, remind them that the boundaries exist because of the strength and impact words have on people's hearts and minds. 'Celia, I know that you are upset right now. But your words have power all the time and I expect you to be careful with them no matter what you are feeling.'

Feedback

Feedback is one of the most important steps. We can help our children to see the impact they have on their own lives, on the lives of others and in the world. Often we do feedback by giving praise and approval, or criticism, but I suggest that an essential shift of feedback is more helpful: moving away from our personal opinion and towards helping children to use their eyes to see their own impact. When talking about the power of words, for example, feedback can look like this:

- When boundaries are broken, frame for them the negative impact the words they use are having on the people and situations around them. Words carry the power to change not only others, but our circumstances as well. 'Sweetie, have you ever noticed that sometimes other kids get frustrated when you are all playing together? Did you know that every time one of your friends suggested changing the game, your voice and words communicated to them that you didn't like their idea and didn't want to play like that? I think that made people begin to feel unsafe and unloved around you. Is that what you wanted to happen? How can you use your words to include people and make your play time joy-filled instead of stress-filled?'
- Watch out for occasions when your children use their words brilliantly and notice the impact it is having. 'I noticed you shielded your friend from those children who were trying to hurt him with their words. That was brave and kind.'
- Give feedback about the impact their words have on you. 'When you told me that I am not fat, that really made me realise how much I say that! You are right! I'm not fat, and it's not good for me to keep saying that to myself. Thanks for helping me see that.'

This circle enables us not only to create the behaviours we are hoping to see but also to create the deeply held values that lie underneath. Throughout this book, we will be using this tool to explore different ways to disciple children in their purpose, easily and lightly. The more familiar we become with this simple way of harnessing our influence, the more we will see the spiritual fruit in our children's lives.

*

— Chapter 4 —

Foundational purpose

In the novel *The Lord of the Rings*, there was a quest. An evil enemy was attempting to conquer the land, and the good guys had discovered the way to defeat him. An essential journey had to be undertaken in order to destroy an object for the good of all the world. A core group of people from different societies were so captivated by this purpose, by the fundamental goodness of its goal, that they voluntarily chose to sacrifice all to achieve it. The quest required them to shine individually, to support each other, and to sacrifice personal goals for the good of their purpose. Sometimes alone and sometimes together, the core group finally achieved their grand purpose and saved the world.

What would have happened if one of the characters had refused to participate until he was individually given a plan for exactly what would be required of him on this quest? What would have happened if they stopped each time a question or crisis arose, or waited until someone told them exactly what to do based on their individual strengths and weaknesses?

The reason the core group achieved their purpose was that their eyes were fixed on that grand purpose. They applied themselves to achieve that goal, in community with each other. Together they were stronger than when they were apart, and it needed each one of them to succeed.

Throughout scripture there is a whole host of purposes outlined for people following God. Jesus simplified it beautifully for us: '"Love the Lord your God with all your heart and with all your soul and with all your mind." This is the first and greatest commandment. And the second is like it: "Love your neighbour as yourself." All the Law and the Prophets hang on these two commandments' (Matthew 22:37–40).

When Jesus came to earth, he lived that purpose, and we see the power that a life lived well can truly have. Jesus brought God's love to earth, and that love set people free and brought joy and fulfilment and healing to a broken world, reconciling people to God. When he returned to heaven, he tasked his followers with doing the same as he had done.

It is this purpose that we need to own for ourselves, this purpose that will fulfil us and give us a goal each day of our lives. Too often we dismiss that grander purpose as too impersonal, while we are waiting for God to give us our own individual detailed step-by-step plan.

For a long time I searched for my calling, the unique plan that God had for my life, the journey that was designed for me and my wonderfulness. To be honest, I dismissed the purposes laid out in scripture because I found them boring.

I looked at scripture and was overwhelmed by the list of things to do: act justly, love mercy, serve the poor, take care of widows and orphans, proclaim the good news, set captives free, bring sight to the blind, make disciples of all nations, destroy the works of the enemy, visit those in prison, clothe the naked, feed the hungry... That couldn't be my purpose!

I had confused the commands in scripture with purpose. In my head, purpose had been reduced to dos and don'ts. Purpose was robbed of power and replaced with obligation and obedience. I found no appeal in that. I wanted to know my destiny, not a list of things that everyone should do.

I think that is common for many of us. We look first to see our path in the midst of the grander purpose, and by doing so, we miss out. When we choose to follow Christ, we choose to be part of the core team set to achieve the purposes of God on this earth. And what are those? Nothing less than the rescuing of each individual in the world, the breaking of the darkness over people's lives and the reconciliation between them and their Father, a restoration of his kingdom on earth.

No matter what job or ministry we have, this purpose will still stand. No matter what particular calling the Lord gives to us or spiritual gifts we receive, they will be a part of this purpose, and that is wonderful.

All the dos and don'ts detailed in scripture are to help us understand how to pursue that purpose and be effective in it. I do believe that God has specific tasks for us to accomplish as part of the grander purpose, and we will be talking about that in Chapter 8. Growing in our children the foundational purpose of love and freedom we are all called to is absolutely crucial to their ability to feel and be effective and purposeful each day. Without this understanding of our foundational purpose, our children can feel paralysed and unsatisfied in their search for what God wants them to do.

So how do we train our children to embrace and pursue this purpose Jesus passed to them? In the next four chapters we will be exploring how to help our children:

- to see how powerful they really are
- to live a life of compassion and courage
- to run their individual path well and confidently

*

— Chapter 5 —

Seeing power in the mirror

At a weekend away, the children were having their own time to connect with God in prayer, and a nine-year-old girl beckoned me over to tell me about her time with God. She told me that while she was chatting with God, a picture popped up in her mind of his giving her a crown at school for her to wear. As the story progressed in her mind, she walked around with the crown on her head, and people moved out of the way and listened to what she had to say. She told me that she thought it was because God is a king and her father, and we chatted a bit about what that means in scripture. I asked her if she felt God was asking her to do something specific with the influence he has given her as his child. Instantly her thoughts went to a 'weird' girl who had no friends and was very lonely. She talked about how she could totally change how that girl feels every day if she decided to be faithful friends with her and connect her into other friends.

A shadow crossed her face. 'What if she becomes really clingy because she doesn't have other friends? What if my friends don't like her because she is weird and they stop being my friend because of it?' I nodded and told her that there is a lot to weigh up when choosing what to do. Her face wrinkled up. 'Oh gosh, it is hard sometimes having so much power and responsibility as the child of the king, isn't it?' I assured her that it is, sometimes. After a pause, she nodded solemnly and said, with a smile spreading across her face, 'I choose to change her life. This is going to be gooooood.'

We live in a world that tends to disempower children. Our culture communicates that power comes through titles and roles, through being a 'leader' or controlling our environment or our peers. Social status and being famous give us power, our culture says. Physical intimidation gives us power. Being the smartest, the prettiest, the strongest are all ways to gain what we don't have: power. Children want to play with the right toys, to dress in a certain way, to fit in and be clever, or louder or less weird or anything else that will allow other people to find value in them. They feel the pressure to change themselves to what other people like so that they can be endowed with power by others.

What our children often don't understand is that they are powerful without all those things. They were given power when they were created and have been given a powerful identity because of their relationship with God. They have somehow been lied to about how powerful they are, and so they chase after regaining something they never lost.

The first step towards building purposeful children is to shape powerful ones. This process is about helping children to discover their natural power as people, and then linking their understanding of how powerful they are to who God made them to be on this earth. They need to be trained to see power in the mirror, to be able to look at themselves and see a powerful person, and to be equipped to know how to use it well. Purpose is just a directed application of the power they already have.

Too often we try to push children into purpose when they don't understand how powerful they are. This leads them to feel inadequate and stressed, feeling the 'shoulds' press on them to perform religion well instead of confidently living who they truly are.

For children to understand power, they have to know that who they are matters as well as what they do. They need to know that:

- I am heavy: my presence carries weight
- My voice is powerful
- I am an influential follower
- I have spiritual power and authority because I am God's child

I am heavy: my presence carries weight

Often children and young people are used to being the 'add-on' to the more powerful people in the room. Usually these people are the adults or the natural leaders among their peers. They have learned that other people are the ones who decide if they are or aren't valuable and significant in a certain context. They have to wait to be given power by the people who hold it.

Some of this is a right understanding of how certain social situations work, and that is perfectly proper. We do not always have the position to speak or influence in situations. If I attended Prime Minister's Questions in the gallery, I would not have the right to speak because I have not been given that position. While there is a right teaching of respect and position, though, sometimes children can internalise that to help shape their identity as *always powerless* unless someone gives them power.

Children need to know the many ways that they are *always significant*, which is the power they carry just by being themselves. I describe it to children this way: they are heavy. This heaviness comes from being a creation of God. They were designed with the ability to be powerful.

Sometimes children feel as if they are a feather. They can't really make a difference to the societal or spiritual scales either way. But when we teach our children to view themselves as having weight, they begin to learn that where they put this weight can shift the balance and make a huge difference. Their weight can tip the scales.

They need to know that when they are part of a crowd, they still can have an impact. They don't stop being who they are because they are in a crowd. When they are in a room and something wrong is happening, simply by standing by they are saying that they approve and agree that it's OK. When we agree with people, we add weight to their choices.

Children need to know what to do with their weight when they are in a large group. If they think they are a feather, it's easy for them to go along with the wind. If they think of themselves like a lead weight, they have to make a choice to move their weight.

This is the way I often talk children through a scenario of being in a large group: 'Sometimes, when you are in a group, you choose to put your weight behind the leader. But if your group starts to discuss or do things that squish your integrity, what should you do? 1) Use your voice and then 2) decide where to put your weight. If people want to do something with which you don't agree, put your weight somewhere else. You can be the one who says, "No thanks, I'm going to go over here and do something else." If a group is bullying, then you can move your weight over to the one who needs help. Be the one who stands next to him and tells the bullies to back off, or invite the child to leave and play with you.'

I tell children that if you stay part of a crowd, you have chosen to keep your weight there, and you are responsible for the power you have added to it.

My voice is powerful

As babies begin to talk, they grow in their understanding of the usefulness of words. As they grow older, though, life can teach them that their words are not valuable or powerful when dealing with other people. In order for children to feel able to affect the world around them, they must feel confident that their voices, their words, are influential.

The truth is that everyone's voice is intrinsically powerful. You don't have to be in charge to be influential. That's why what we say matters so much. Encouragement and compliments lift people up, and insults and mean observations hurt. Scripture talks about how our tongues are like a spark that can start a forest fire (James 3:1–12). Solomon went so far as to say words can bring death or life (Proverbs 18:21). Part of human design is that the words we speak out about ourselves and others impact on other people's self-perceptions and relationships and on society itself.

Each one of our children has a powerful voice. Their opinions, insights, thoughts and ideas are valuable and important, even in disagreement. They have a unique view that needs to be heard and counselled with, and it is important that they learn to use their powerful voice responsibly and positively.

I am an influential follower

Our children can sometimes feel that unless they are the leader, they are nothing. I believe that this is because we haven't trained them in the immense power of being a follower. Derek Sivers drew our attention to this phenomenon at a TED conference (see http://sivers.org/ff). He showed a YouTube video taken at a music festival. There was a sea of thousands of people sitting and listening to a performance on the side of a large hill, and on the fringes of the crowd was a man. He was a tiny, skinny man in little shorts dancing with ridiculous and complete abandonment, like I used to do as a child in front of my mirror in my bedroom. This man was on his own, having a great time, while thousands of people rolled their eyes and judged him. He did this for over half an hour, just as wacky, just as weird, totally revelling in the music.

And then it happened. One guy leaped up out of the crowd and joined him. He didn't join in shyly; he went for it, just like the original dancer. About 30 or 40 seconds later, a second man joined, and then five and then 20 and then 80 and in the span of three minutes, over a hundred people were dancing and laughing and having a great time surrounding this man, dancing just like him. As that song ended, a huge cheer went up and they lifted the original dancer in the air.

Derek Sivers asked the questions: what made the difference? What created this moment? In his view, it was the first follower. The first follower turned the wacky guy into a leader. He showed others how to follow and broke down barriers for others to join in. The second follower was also important and the subsequent followers added momentum, but it took a lot of bravery for the first follower in particular to throw his weight in with the original lone dancer. The first follower's choice changed the dance of one man into a movement.

We see this in scripture over and over again, but never more so than with Jesus' disciples. Jesus was one man doing great things, but it was his disciples, empowered by the Holy Spirit, who took his message around the world. Being a follower is a powerful thing.

Our children need to know that they are just as powerful when they are a follower. They can add their weight to someone or something and make a huge difference.

They can be the first follower. Who do they see at church, at school or in the community who is doing something good but needs someone to believe in her, to join her, to have someone add weight to her voice? What ministry needs their support financially or physically? What lonely child with a great idea needs someone to go to his meeting? Who is God asking our children to stand by and be the best follower there is? Rather than thinking, 'Who else will be there?', could they think, 'What would I add if I went?'

I have spiritual power and authority because I am God's child

When we know who we are, we naturally live by the permission and authority that this gives. A child knows the rules of the house and also knows the permissions of the house granted to her because of who she is. She can walk into the house, dump her clothes in her room, grab some food, plonk down on the sofa and whack on the TV because it is her home—not because she did anything to earn it, but because she is her parent's child. That identity gives her authority to live in her home and special permission to access most of it.

Children know how this feels, because every day they act as your children. They know what that requires, what permission they have, and what authority they carry because of it. My dad was a police officer as well as an instructor at the police academy. As a teen and young adult, I could confidently walk through the gates of the police academy and into rooms with intimidating men and seas of cadets and feel totally comfortable—not because I had any right to be there or do anything, but because of who my dad was and the identity I had through him. I had a right to be there because of my father. It was his authority of which I was able to be a part.

When we came into Christ, we became children of God. Our identity as children of God gives us not only access to our Father but also a confidence in the freedom and permission we have because of who he is, not because of who we are.

When Jesus was ministering on earth, he had the authority that his father gave him. 'All authority in heaven and on earth has been given to me,' Jesus said (Matthew 28:18). Because of his authority and the power of the Holy Spirit that empowered him, he worked out his purpose on earth, accomplishing great things. Then Jesus gave his authority to us, and now we can do the same.

Our children can have a solid sense of identity and authority in Christ in order to accomplish what God has called them to accomplish on this earth.

When our children know that they have weight, that their voices are powerful, that they are influential followers and that they are children of God who carry spiritual authority, then they are able to work out their purpose by simply choosing where to apply the power they know they have.

The six-stage circle

So as parents, how can we instil these truths in our children? Let's explore some ideas as we take them round the six-stage circle.

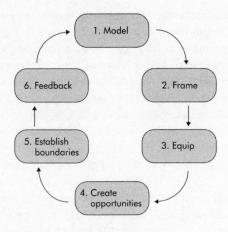

Model

Tell stories of times when you were in a crowd and disagreed with what was happening. What did you do, and why? How did you feel about it? How do you think God felt about it?

When you are all together as a family, let your children see you being 'heavy' and making a difference. Help a struggling single mother to load her car with her groceries, help a family move, give a homeless man your umbrella even if it is raining and this leaves you wet, cook meals for a grieving family. Let them see you making a difference in people's lives, just by being there for others when no one else is.

Let them see you use your voice in powerful ways. Deflect some gossip or defend someone who needs it. Encourage and build up someone who is upset or praise others in their failure. Let your children see the impact a voice can make on people and situations.

Do some reflecting on your experiences as a follower. Where are you adding your weight? Where are you going for the purpose of following well or for being that key follower who adds momentum?

Invite your children along. Create a window for them to hear your feelings about it and why you go.

Create windows into how you live as a child of God. Chat to God informally in front of them. Share your favourite worship song or Bible story. Tell them a story of when you first realised what it meant to be a child of God.

Pray for people in front of your children, so they can learn what it means to pray with authority as God's child.

Frame

When you are heading to attend a meeting, frame the power of your presence, your heaviness. 'I really want to go because it's important for Susie to see that I support her. I want to be a positive person in the room to help other people join in. What she is doing is important, and I want to add my weight to what she is doing. I can really help by going.'

Wonder out loud about the people in the Bible who used their weight to tip the scales. Daniel was one man disobeying an unjust law (Daniel 6). Shadrach, Meshach and Abednego put their lives on the line to put their weight with God (Daniel 3). Esther weighed in with the king and saved a nation (see the book of Esther). Tell stories of people in the Bible who used their voice powerfully. John the Baptist showed Jesus to people (Matthew 3; Mark 1; Luke 3; John 1). Gamaliel stopped a crowd from killing Peter and a group of disciples just by speaking wisdom (Acts 5:34–40). Jesus' words brought spiritual and emotional freedom to people.

Debrief with your children why you speak the way that you do in certain places. 'Have you ever noticed that when we are at Scouts and your leader says things that you know I disagree with, I just smile? It's because I don't want to embarrass him. Sometimes I chat with him about it afterwards if I think it's important. It's good to make sure that, if we can, we use our voices in a way that doesn't embarrass people.'

Watch movies together and discuss the 'sidekicks' and key followers who empower the leader. Could the leader have accomplished all that hero work without them? Why, or why not? Why don't followers get as much attention?

Go to places with your child, and instead of chatting with the leaders, chat with the key followers. Praise them in front of your children and acknowledge their key roles.

Point out when people are being the first followers or part of an initial group. Notice how the situation changes because of what they do. Notice when a situation really needed a first follower to participate in order to take off, but no one stepped up. How did the leader feel? How would it have been different if followers had joined in?

Verbally frame aspects of your relationship with God when you act out of that place of God-connection. For example, before you head into nanny and grandad's house, take a minute to pray as a family, thanking God for being your Father and asking that he come with you into the house so that they may know him better through you.

Equip

Chat over possible scenarios that would require your children to make a tough decision about where they put their weight. While you are doing dishes or driving around, pose hypothetical situations and ask what they think they would do. 'When I was your age, I went to the toilet at school and found three children making fun of a little child while he washed his hands. I'm not sure I handled it very well. What do you think you would do in that situation? What are the choices?' There is no right answer to these questions, but it can help your children to work through all the different scenarios. They could ignore it and just go to the toilet. They could distract the bullies by asking a question. They could join the small child and wash their hands and leave with him, and be able to use their powerful voice to encourage. They could tell the bullies to stop and defend the small child. They could leave and get a teacher. They could just leave and do nothing. There are many choices, with different consequences for each. Have a great conversation!

Wonder out loud what makes a good follower. Invite the curate or assistant minister to your home and ask about his or her journey in that supporting role.

Plan together to attempt to be the best followers ever during something (sports practice, church, Scouts) and then discuss how it went. What worked? What didn't? How did it feel?

Notice when your children are following well or bravely choosing to be a first follower or part of an initial group. Help them to see the impact it made on other people.

Continue to help your children develop a deeper heart-to-heart connection with God. Ask them about how it feels to do life with God together, and chat with them about all the precious moments you cherish with God throughout the day. Suggest that they find a similar moment with God each day.

Create opportunities

As a family, stop when you enter church, look around and decide if there is any place that needs your family's weight. Is there a new family that could use some companionship? Is there a family with several young children that could use some extra hands during worship?

Come home from a tough day and ask your child's advice on a work scenario. 'Someone at work is very cranky and is hurting people with her words. I want to say or do something to help the situation, but I haven't quite figured out what. What do you think?' Ask follow-up questions and chat about the consequences of the possibilities. Don't forget to give feedback once you do something about it!

Help your children to spot opportunities to be excellent followers for someone. Help them to find some cause that touches their hearts and to which they would want to add their weight. Encourage them to pursue it or offer to go with them. This could be anything from hearing a friend mention a good idea to solve a problem at school, to being moved to go on a mission trip. It could be volunteering to join a team on a new ministry at church or writing encouragement letters to persecuted Christians in China. The more you expose your child to good leaders with passion, the more their hearts will have the variety to chime with!

Invite your children along to be influential followers in something you are leading. Chat before the event about where you need support and how they could help the situation. After the event, help your children to see how they influenced other people to engage by being brilliant followers. Express your gratitude and appreciation.

When your child has a nightmare, remind her that as a child of God, he is with her always. God is right next to her, and so she can tell the dreams to go away in the name of Jesus because she is God's child. Share with her that the Bible says that 'perfect love drives out fear' (1 John 4:18) and invite God to hug your child and sweep all the fear away.

Expose your child to needs in your community and in the world, and suggest that you would support her if she wanted to add her weight to do something about it. Coach her through the process of finding out more information, planning a way to help and accomplishing her goal: this could be anything from a collection for orphans in Uganda, to gathering toys for the poor in your town, to a sponsored silence for a disabled child at her school, to visiting the elderly at Christmas.

Establish boundaries

How do you want to guide your children in the development of understanding their own power? What are the boundaries for their behaviour? Some parents set boundaries for their children's external behaviour. It might look like this: 'If you are part of a group or being a follower, then you should do it well. If you can't keep your integrity as part of a group, we can give you some time off to think about how you want to deal with those situations when you return.' Maybe it is simply watching your children's internal development and knowing when you want to step in to coach a bit more. If you notice that a particular group or leader is making your children feel powerless and out of control, then you might want to step in to coach your children to find their voice again. If you see them standing by while something bad happens, do you want to hold them accountable for adding their implicit weight to it, or, rather, ask them what they did about the situation?

Check the messages that are going into your child's head from both the secular and Christian scenarios of which they are part. Is your child being surrounded by the message that power is found in violence or in beauty? Are the media that he watches reinforcing his God-given power or redefining it? Are the friends she is playing with making her feel powerful or powerless?

Children are designed to be part of God's plan on this earth. It is part of how they were created. They have the power to impact people's physical, emotional, mental and spiritual lives significantly. We want them to know this for themselves, but we also need to ensure that they understand that all of this is true of others. As they learn how to exercise their power, they will need to learn how to respect and honour other people's power as well. Many of your house rules may naturally fall within this idea: 'Please don't pull at your brother. He has chosen not to play and we respect people's decision to say no. Why don't you go and play and we'll see where he chooses to be.' 'Please don't yell over people. It is important that everyone's voice is allowed to be powerful. We don't use our powerful voices to squish others.' 'Please be careful of your bossiness. Your friends chose to be followers when they said "yes" to your game, but it is important to honour our followers and treat them well. They could choose to follow someone else.'

Feedback

Raising our children to be powerful people requires them to have a safe place to be part of a consistent and loving feedback loop. Our families are the perfect places for this to happen.

Would our parenting change if we treated our children as significant people whose presence and voice carried weight in our lives and in our family? Could we consult them more or ask their opinion? Often we just get on with life, taking all the decisions for our family, big and small. Our children get used to not having a voice in the group of our family, with the power resting solely with the parents. How can we adjust our parenting so that we still hold leadership without disempowering our children? Here are some ideas.

Notice and acknowledge when they enter a room. Look up, smile, wave and pat them on the back. Let them know you see them and are glad they are there. Often we spend significant chunks of our time with our children while tuning them out. Let them know that their presence is important to you.

Give your children significant roles in an activity. Arrange it so that their contribution makes a difference or that the task would have been harder if they hadn't been there. After the activity is done, be specific about how they not only helped you but also enabled other benefits. For instance, by helping you to shop, the errand went faster, so you had more time to be peaceful, and the whole family was less stressed. The result: they helped to change the home atmosphere by helping you. Or, because they planned and cooked a meal for you, you were able to meet up with a struggling friend and help her through a difficult time. The result: their powerfulness enabled a person they don't know to feel blessed. When we not only let them help us but also show them the impact of their efforts, then we remove the 'just' word from their sentences ('I'm *just* a helper, not a leader,' 'I *just* pushed the trolley'). They will begin to learn that their weight added to the whole, so that they were a part of the result.

Allow your children to come up with the solutions to their own problems. Instead of rushing to help or sorting it for them, say, 'Oh no! What are you going to do?' This communicates to your children that you are confident that they are able to respond to a difficult situation.

Choose situations during the day in which your child can participate in the decision-making. For instance, invite your child to run errands with you and give them the choice of which shop to visit first, or ask their advice on what vegetable to serve for dinner. Ask their opinion about situations *and take their advice*. Often we ask their opinion and then ignore it or do something different. From little to large situations, the more you genuinely allow them to influence decisions, the more comfortable they will be in their voice having power and in the consequences this will have.

Make your home a place for your child to exercise her authority as a child of God. Empower her relationship with God daily and give her the honour of leading the family in prayer at the Christmas meal.

*

— Chapter 6 —

Learning the way of love

I was praying with nine-year-old Lucy, who was being badly bullied. She came to pray with me that God would stop the verbal abuse. We prayed for God to help heal Lucy's heart from the mean words spoken to her, and for God to protect her at school. As we chatted together afterwards, I mentioned that often people become bullies because something is going on in their lives. I gently suggested that if she was up for it, she could ask God about it. She looked surprised at the idea and wanted to ask him right then.

We sat back down and she settled in. She asked God what was going on in the bully's life. In the silence that followed, God showed her a picture of the bully sitting alone on the ground in the middle of a field, bleeding, next to a fallen bike, and her family far away laughing at her. Lucy was disturbed that no one was helping her, and she felt that God was showing her how the other girl felt lonely, unloved and hurt. Something welled up in Lucy as she told me about what God had showed her. She said, 'I just want to pray some more right now.'

As I sat next to her, she prayed earnestly for about ten minutes, asking God to give friends to the lonely and hurt girl, to help her feel God's love and smile, to change her life circumstances and to heal her hurt heart. When Lucy finished, she was totally changed. She was no longer focused on the hurt of being bullied but was filled with compassion for this other child. She sat and thought for a bit and decided that she was going to make it her goal to show this other child that she was loveable. 'I know that she will probably just keep being mean to me, but I will keep reminding myself of how she feels inside. I won't let her hurt me or push me, but I'm not going to ignore her or be mean back. I'll still protect me, but I'm also going to attack her with niceness and love. All year. Someone needs to make her feel that she isn't alone.'

We must remember that at the root of purpose is simple love. Jesus answered the question 'Which is the greatest commandment?' with 'Love the Lord your God with all your heart and with all your soul and with all your mind,' but he did not finish there. He went on to summarise the rest of the law as 'Love your neighbour as yourself' (Matthew 22:37–40). 'Neighbour' here literally means anyone you have anything to do with. To Jesus, expressing love for God is inextricably linked with loving others. Ignoring or retreating from the world is simply not an option. Multi-directional love is at the very centre of the Christian purpose.

Cultivating our 'heart garden'

In our modern Christianity we have begun, wrongly, to separate the idea of 'acting lovingly' from the concept of actual 'love'. 'Love is an action,' I have heard said in churches. 'We don't need to feel full of love to act out of love.' In another sermon I heard, 'We can't just wait for the fuzzy feeling of the emotion of love to come; sometimes we just need to act lovingly first.' I even read in a children's curriculum: 'Love is a choice, not an emotion.'

I think this separation is a false one. This concept has allowed God's command to love to become mere religious duty. When it says in scripture that God is love or that God's love is abounding and everlasting, it is not talking about him just acting lovingly without feeling it. When Jesus walked on the earth, he didn't merely act as if he loved people. I believe that the heart of the Father, the Son and the Spirit is love. I believe that when we were commanded to love God and others, it was a genuine command to cultivate a heart full of love from which our actions would naturally flow.

I am responsible before God to love him authentically from the depths of my soul and being, and to love my neighbour authentically from that same place. It is my job as a parent, with the help of the Spirit, to tend my heart garden to produce the fruit of love—to remove the weeds that choke the growth of love, to feed and provide for the nourishment of my love, and to protect and guard it so that it doesn't become scarred or unusable. It is my job to ensure that what my heart grows and pours out *through* my choices and actions is love.

So often we tell our children to think of what would be the loving thing to do in a situation and then to do it. This isn't what God is talking about. In every situation, we are called to *love*, not just to perform. Love isn't a thought process. Love isn't an action first. It is a heart attitude, a spiritual fruit of a walk with our Father. Love is an emotion; a powerful, motivating energy generator that powers our actions. If we disconnect that generator, if we deny the necessity of the motivational cultivation, we are left merely with striving and religious duty, attempting to fulfil tasks he never gave us.

We are called to love the way Jesus loved. We need to start noticing how he cultivated his heart, instead of how to replicate his actions.

When a conflict arises between children, we often try to help them problem-solve what to do. We focus on their behaviour instead of their heart. When the name-calling or the shoving starts, we often try to stop this behaviour and reinforce better behaviour. All well and good, but how often do we pull our child aside and say, 'What's going on with your heart? It seems that it only took a little thing for you to get very angry with Daniel. Why do you think you are so angry? What pushed the love away?' It is our job to help our children to learn to reconcile and live with a heart of love instead of a muddled heart of anger, pain, fear or stress.

It is our job as parents not only to grow in our children a heart of compassion, but also to give them a worldview of love. It is our job to teach our children how to be in charge of their own heart gardens. Too often our children feel victims of the world. People hurt them and disappoint them and their hearts get battered, and their only way to fix it is to lash out or strike back or shut others out or try to control the other person. We are able to coach our children in how to defend their hearts well, maintain love with strength and forgive others in order to keep their hearts in a healthy state. It is training our children to pause before they act; to notice that 'I'm filled with hurt and bitterness towards this person' and sort that heart position out first. It's restoring love before they act lovingly, instead of the other way around.

Why? Because real love is transformational for all involved. The Bible tells us that love chases away all fear (1 John 4:18), and causes us to lay down our lives for each other (John 15:13). It is how we will be known to the world (13:35) and it is how Jesus provided a way for us to reconcile with the Father and how he bought freedom for us (3:16). Love is at the core of how we as humans respond. It is the key to our hearts and to this broken world.

So if we are called to love as Jesus loved, how did he cultivate his heart garden, and how can we do that with our children? Scripture gives us some clues of how Jesus grew and operated out of a pure love for his Father and for others. He:

- drew close to God
- saw people through God's eyes
- maintained compassion for people and loved them as himself
- walked in forgiveness

Drawing close to God

When Jesus' disciple John was talking about love, he pointed directly to the source of all love:

'My dear friends, we must love each other. Love comes from God, and when we love each other, it shows that we have been given new life. We are now God's children, and we know him. God is love, and anyone who

doesn't love others has never known him… We love because God loved us first.' (1 John 4:7–8, 19, CEV)

Jesus often carved out time to spend with God, one to one. He went to his Father for comfort and counsel, to worship him and to draw near to him (see Mark 1:35; 6:45–46; 14:32–34; Luke 5:16). Throughout his life, Jesus was so aware of the presence of his Father that he told his disciples that he did only what he saw his Father doing (John 5:19). Jesus rooted himself in the knowledge, presence and love of his Father.

It is absolutely essential that children know the intensity of emotion the Father feels for them, especially children who come from broken circumstances or painful home lives. They must also understand that God's love is expressed in an active pursuit of us. It is expressed in Jesus' laying aside his majesty and coming to dwell with us; in giving up his life on the cross to reconcile us; in reaching out in acts of mercy throughout history in order to see lives transformed.

Children need to know that because of what Jesus did, we can be God's children and experience a personal and daily life with him filled with his joy, presence and love. They deserve to grow to know God and his love for them deep in their being, so that they can't be shaken from it by the world. This is so important that I spent an entire book, *Parenting Children for a Life of Faith*, exploring how we as parents can empower our children to live in a vibrant, two-way relationship with God.

When children are God-connected and not just God-smart, their understanding of love comes to life. Since God is the essence of love, the best way to define it for them is to connect them in relationship with him! If love flows out of our relationship with God and how we see each other in the light of this, love is a worldview to cultivate, not a rule to enforce.

Seeing people through God's eyes

When Jesus met people, he rarely responded to what he saw with his own eyes. Most of the time, he saw people through his Father's eyes as precious, lost, needy and loved. Often he would hear his Father speak specifics about people's lives, hearts and circumstances, even before the people themselves shared them.

Jesus was able to love people extraordinarily because he saw them through the eyes of the one who loved them most.

We can empower children's purpose by helping them to learn to see people and situations from God's viewpoint. It is so hard in our humanness to understand, but God's view is different from ours. 'People look at the outward appearance, but the Lord looks at the heart' (1 Samuel 16:7). To us, situations and people can look broken and messy, mean or unfixable. We can see no way forward with our own eyes. God sees differently.

God looks at people's hearts. He sees the whole: the actions and what is deep in the hearts of those who act. When we choose to look from his point of view, we can begin to understand how to love people.

For children, I find it helpful to explain that God has the ability to see into the very centre of people's hearts and minds. That he loves each person on earth deeply and faithfully. That it makes his heart ache with sadness when he sees the people he created hurting each other, suffering, and getting lost in sin and darkness. That he longs to set each one free from all brokenness and give them a hope and a future. I encourage children to go to God with their questions about people and situations, so that they can talk together about how to love best.

It is our honour as parents to be able to frame for our children how to see, not only with our eyes but with God's eyes. We can help them to learn to pause and consider who the person in front of them is to God and then respond out of that understanding. It is also important to be mindful to coach them in how to protect themselves emotionally, spiritually and physically while still loving people with the love of God.

Developing compassion for people

Compassion is a key part of God's heart. Over and over in scripture, we see that compassion is essential to Jesus' character and motivates him to intervene in people's lives. When Jesus walked on earth, he was often moved by compassion to heal or feed or teach.

Compassion comes from understanding and empathising with someone's situation. It requires allowing oneself to hear, see and truly understand what another person is going through and to be emotionally moved in response to it. This natural trait is something that is being eroded by our society and its values. The media allow us to watch people's suffering as entertainment through movies, television crime programmes and children's cartoons. Violence, verbal abuse, rudeness and bullying are all sources of enjoyment as we laugh our way through some 'light entertainment'.

On the playground our boys try to enforce toughness because they don't want to be seen as soft or 'girly', and our girls often get sucked into using emotional and verbal abuse and manipulation with each other.

Compassion isn't a gender issue or an entertainment issue. I'm not arguing that everyone needs to shelter their children in a media-free environment. What I am saying is that compassion is a crucial part of God's character and one of Jesus' main motivations; therefore, it is up to us to shape and help to guide our children in valuing it and operating out of it. It takes deliberation on our part to protect and grow our children's compassion for others.

Walking in forgiveness

Forgiveness was a major theme in Jesus' teachings and in how he lived his life. Jesus even shared with his disciples that before they offered gifts and prayers to God, they needed to forgive others (Mark 11:25; Matthew 5:23). He urged them to sort out their heart gardens on the spot, even in the midst of praying. For Jesus, forgiveness wasn't an occasional thing but a continual process of weeding. Even while experiencing the agony of crucifixion, he still managed to ensure his heart was right and asked his Father to forgive those who were hurting him.

Forgiveness is a big part of maintaining a heart garden of love, and we need to ensure that we are training our children in it well.

I describe forgiveness to children like this: if someone broke into your house and stole your stuff, you do not get to go and find him and then kick him in the shins over and over again until you feel he has been punished enough. If someone broke into your house, what would happen? He would be arrested by the police. The punishment for his crime, the consequence for his actions, would be given to him by our justice system. He would be put in prison or made to pay a fine. You would not get to punish the person. Even though the person stole your things, it is the justice system's job to punish, not ours.

When people do bad things to us, something inside us wants to punish them. We want to hurt them back and be the ones to do it. But God says that that is not our job. He is the one who deals with justice. He is the only one who gets to judge people.

So what can you do? First of all, if you are hurt, or if a crime has happened, you need to tell an adult. God put parents, teachers, church leaders and governments there to keep people safe and to help carry out his justice. But what do we do with our hearts and our relationship with others?

Well, we can keep carrying around our emotions, wanting to punish those people and trying to hurt them and get at them, or we can let God help to heal our hearts and trust him to be the judge of those people. We can trust that God will judge them. It's our job not to let that hurt and fear and upsetness damage our heart garden and interfere with the love we are growing or with our ability to live our purpose on earth. Those things can choke our joy and happiness and love. We need to forgive, not because other people deserve it, but because God wants us to live free and humbly before him, letting God be God. Forgiving means saying to yourself and to God, 'I am really hurt and upset, God. What happened to me wasn't right. But I leave it with you to deal with, whichever way you want to. I let go of my anger and my desire to hurt them back. God can help to heal my heart garden so that I can live a life of love and joy and peace again.'

Jesus' ability to forgive and love was so great that he not only didn't desire to punish the people who hurt him, but he even asked God not to punish them. True forgiveness allows love to triumph over all. Because of the lifestyle of love and forgiveness Jesus lived, he was able to fulfil his purpose to bring us freedom from sin and death.

The six-stage circle

So how do we begin to cultivate our children's heart gardens and train our children to maintain their heart gardens for the sake of living out their purpose on earth? Let's explore some practical ideas through the six-stage circle.

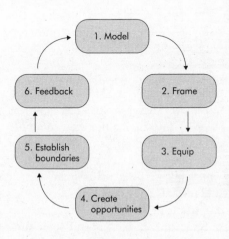

Model

Allow your children to see you on your journey of loving God. Let them peek into how you chat with him and access his voice. Talk about your feelings about God and how life with him works. Display to them what an authentic everyday relationship with God looks like, not a fantasy of an ideal one.

Voice your thoughts out loud about people you encounter, sharing how you can see them with God's eyes. As you walk past the homeless man on your road, smile at him and ask how he is getting on. As you walk away, say briefly to your children, 'God loves that man a lot. I was praying for him the other day on the bus.'

Occasionally let your children see some of the ordinary sacrifices of compassion and love that happen in your everyday life. Often our children don't know that you do these things, but unless they see a glimmer of it, they don't know that it's part of the average everyday life of a follower of Jesus. Let them see you opt to buy a cheaper meal for the family so that you can buy a 'special extra' as a gift for someone at church.

Tell stories of when you were wronged and either forgave someone or didn't forgive. Share your experience and the impact your choices made on you and others.

Frame

Be aware of when you tune in to God throughout the day or week. Notice when and how it happens. Share about that experience with your child. 'You know, I never noticed before, but my best times with God are when I am just chatting with him in the shower.' If you think your child is receptive, ask, 'When do you think about God or chat with him?' Don't worry about 'teaching' the answer or correcting your child. This is just to frame experiences, not to nudge your child towards compliance.

While you are sitting in a public place waiting, lean over to your child and ask, 'Who do you see?' Spend some fun time people-watching the way you normally do. Then ask, 'God sees people a bit differently. How you do think he sees these same people? What about that man?' If you are both feeling brave, you can ask God directly, 'How do you see that woman in the green coat?' Sometimes you may feel that you want to pray quickly for that person as you watch him or her walk around.

Verbalise when something hits your heart on the news, in your family or circle of friends, or as you walk around. When you drive past a car accident, instead of just saying, 'Oh, here we go. That's what the problem was!' take a moment outwardly to process the flicker of compassion that happens internally as well. 'Oh, here we go. That's what the problem was! Gosh, look. Those people are standing out in the cold and their car is crunched up. They must be feeling very scared, cold and shaken. God, please send your peace to surround them and help them.'

Sometimes conflicts in our friendships or marriages happen in front of our children, but the making-up happens somewhere else. How to resolve conflict and forgiveness healthily is something that often children don't see. On the occasions when your children see part of the conflict, it may be a good opportunity to tell the story of how you resolved the issue and forgave the person. 'Remember the other day when Liz said something that made me feel hurt and I got snappy with her? I'm sorry we did that in front of you. Did that make you feel uncomfortable? Sometimes when my feelings get hurt, I let my words talk out of the wrong place. I was talking out of hurt, not love, and that's never good. I said sorry to Liz, and she said sorry to me. I had to spend some time with God forgiving her, so that next time we chat I'm not thinking, "You said mean things to me," but I can think, "I love Liz." I feel much better now. I just wanted you to know that I'm OK, and Liz and I are getting on fine.'

Equip

Take your children to the local park or to someone's garden and show them how growing a garden works. Maybe invite a friend along who knows about plants and can tell your children about all the work and effort that goes into producing a beautiful garden. Share how our hearts are like gardens, and that it's our job to tend them with God's help so that we can do great things with our lives. We have to be careful what we let grow in our hearts.

When your children are upset about a situation, listen to them and give them compassion and understanding. Validate their feelings, and then ask them: how do they think God sees the situation? Maybe ask God for some wisdom for a way forward. Pray with your children, if they are willing, that God will heal their heart and grow more love that will push out any bad feeling that has taken root in their hearts.

Expose your children to different needs in the world so that they can grow familiar with the struggles people have. Watch documentaries, visit museums or look in magazines. Chat about other people's lives and draw parallels between their experiences and yours. Ponder together why people behave as they do, and to what emotions, worries and fears they might be responding. Compassion is empathy, the ability to understand and feel what other people are feeling. It is important to help to train your children to be able to see others' experiences reflected in their own.

Be a positive and loving mirror for your children as they process hurt. As you support them in their journey, notice when they are acting out of hurt and pain. Highlight for them how stressful and painful it is for them, and how it is affecting others. Gently open up a conversation about how they feel, and why they do or don't want to get rid of that anger by forgiving. Listen to their concerns and allow them to go on the journey of forgiveness at their own pace.

Invite your children to join you as you meet up with a mum and her special needs child who is lonely. Share a story of when you were lonely and how you can see that they are feeling the same way now. Chat about how you wished someone had done this for you, and now you can do it for someone else. Whatever you normally do, just create a little window for them to see in.

Avoid pairing up 'forgiveness' with 'getting along'. Often we set up a scenario where one child apologises to the other one, and then we communicate an expectation that forgiveness will happen automatically. If one of our children is moping, we can accidentally try to force him into 'forgiving' his sibling in an effort to end the conflict. Instead, try communicating that it is all right if he is struggling to forgive, but while he is sorting out his feelings between himself and God, you would ask that he is at least polite to his sibling. This enables the child to see the difference between a heart change and the behaviour you expect.

Create opportunities

Resource your children's heart connection to God. If you notice that they love music, buy them a worship CD. If they like reading, get them a devotional or testimony book. Send them to a midweek children's group at church or ask them to journal with you as you do your time with God in the mornings.

Invite your child to be more active in church, seeing people from God's view and helping those who need help to find a place to sit or people to talk to.

Stay tuned into your child when everyday opportunities arise to foster compassion. If there is an older person struggling with his trolley, point it out to your child and ponder how you feel when you are physically struggling. If your child seems to be engaging with the idea, wonder what you both could do to help lift his burden, and do it together. No matter where you are, take the natural opportunities to foster compassion and connect it to action.

You won't need to create opportunities for forgiveness. The world will provide those!

Establish boundaries

Lay a foundation of conversation with your children about 'heart gardens'. Chat to your children about how Jesus once said that the words that come out of our mouths come from the overflow of what is in our hearts (Luke 6:45). Let them know that if you notice their words are telling you and other people that something is not going well in their hearts, then you are going to ask them about it, and you would love to help them sort it out. They won't ever be in trouble about what is happening in their hearts. You are their parent and love every bit of them. You want them to have all the great things God has for them, and that includes freedom, peace, joy, love and happiness in their hearts.

Children can get confused about the difference between forgiveness and trust. When talking through forgiveness with children, it is helpful for them to know that just because they forgive someone doesn't mean they have to trust them again immediately. Some people aren't trustworthy with our hearts or with our belongings. Some people aren't safe to be around or haven't yet earned our trust. Forgiving people who hurt us means that we let go of wanting to punish them. God helps to restore our hearts to the place where we can live our purpose well. Forgiving people does not mean that we stay in a place or relationship with people who hurt us.

Feedback

If you notice your children changing because of their encounters with God and their life walk with him, let them know! 'Son, you have made me feel so loved recently. Thank you so much. It just seems to flow out of your heart.'

Draw your children's attention to the impact they are making on their relationships and on those to whom they minister. Tell stories in front of them of the impact they are making on friends or family members.

Notice when your children do something out of compassion. Don't necessarily thank them, but simply say, 'I saw it when you slowed down while you were playing after school to let your friend win. He had come in last each time, and I saw you wanted him not to feel sad. That was a fine bit of compassion you did right there. Did it work out the way you thought it would?' Invite him to tell you the story of why he chose to do that and what impact he saw. Training children to create their own feedback loops is essential for the inevitable day when you can no longer debrief every situation in life with them.

*

— Chapter 7 —

Finding our calling

I was chatting with ten-year-old Ben over ice cream, and he was conflicted. 'I don't know what I'm supposed to do when I grow up. I'm good at singing, so I guess I could be a pop star or worship leader or something. My mum says I have the gift of helping, so I guess a waiter or whatever? I don't know. I don't have to decide yet, I don't think. I'm still a child, but I want to know.'

Finding our calling, our individual path on our journey of purpose is something that we all ponder. It matters to our children as well as to us. If we can learn how to talk to our children about it and to help them feel confident and peaceful about finding their individual path in life, we will be giving them a huge gift of empowerment.

My family and I love watching sports. There is just something about it that gets me very excited: the variety, the pageantry, the high stakes and the gathering of people from around the world. The event that fascinates me most is the marathon.

Lining up together, a sea of individuals stretch, jump and prepare themselves for the ordeal ahead. They all look the same to me, but they are vastly different. Their journeys to get to this moment in time defy categorisation. The race before them isn't really about beating each other, but running the race they have set out for themselves. Each one will have particular weaknesses to watch out for, strengths to rely on, dangers to overcome, temptations to fight. Their motivations are different, their strategies will vary, but the goal is the same: to complete their own race in their own marathon.

The author of Hebrews talks about our life's journey as something similar. 'Therefore, since we are surrounded by such a great cloud of witnesses, let us throw off everything that hinders and the sin that so easily entangles. And let us run with perseverance the race marked out for us, fixing our eyes on Jesus, the pioneer and perfecter of faith' (Hebrews 12:1–2).

We are all on this journey of a life of faith and purpose, adults and children alike. We run alongside each other.

Problems can arise when we become so focused on discovering our individual path that we forget that the goal of the race ahead has been clearly declared: to stand before God at the end of our lives and look back with him and see that we have run our race well; to have accomplished what God has asked us to do; to have lived a life loving the Lord with all our heart, soul, mind and strength, and loving our neighbour as ourselves. Our children can spend a lifetime ignoring the foundational goal of their lives while trying to search for their individual path.

Look at the disciples and those who followed Jesus. They all came from different places and different life experiences, and they shared the common ground of being with Jesus and being trained by him. After he ascended to heaven, they lived their lives. Their individual paths were vastly different: some were apostles and travelled around the world, some stayed at home and cared for orphans and widows, some continued as parents and husbands living transformational lives at their everyday jobs, some were publicly martyred, some preached to thousands, and some were mothers who raised a generation of children who loved God and lived purposeful lives. All of them shared the same foundational goal, but it looked different for each person. All of them shared the same experience with Jesus and were sent out to live lives of purpose, following Jesus' teachings and being empowered by the Spirit. But their individual paths were very different from each other as they each pursued the goal to the best of their ability.

Children are not all the same. Our children are vastly different from each other, and their paths will turn out to be unique. How can we as parents keep them focused on the foundational goal we are all commanded to pursue, prepare their hearts, and still encourage and support them as they run their individual journeys?

Determining a path

In this highly individualised society, we tend to be very good at self-analysis. We crave it. There are seemingly a billion different ways to categorise people. We seek to know ourselves more and more and, by knowing ourselves, we hope to express ourselves more fully. We have personality tests, magazine quizzes, learning styles, leadership strength tests, compatibility analysis and so on to help us know who we are. The design worlds try to convince us to express ourselves through our clothes, our homes and our choices of music and art.

Self-knowledge and self-expression are seen as essential in our modern world. So naturally an intense desire arises in us to help our children self-analyse spiritually. What are their spiritual gifts? What is their unique path and calling in this life? How do I help them find that? The big questions ring in our children's heads strongly. 'What am I going to do with my life? What is "God's will" for me on this planet? What is my calling?' Often, in Christian circles, we place an emphasis on the unique shape of the individual and the unique 'calling' people have in their lives. The problem is that the answers seem so illusory that the search can paralyse children and teens as they look for their tiny thread in the massive tapestry of the world.

When my son was two, I became the world's best day-bag packer. I could look at what we were going to do on that day and pack the perfect bag to facilitate it. Breakfast on the road, followed by a swimming lesson, followed by a lunch meeting with a volunteer, afternoon shopping, attending a birthday party and then home. No problem. The bag would be perfect, ready to facilitate everything we had to accomplish (adjusting even for what his personality would be like at certain times of day).

My son became accustomed to the magic of the day bag. We would arrive at a location, and before he even asked, the relevant tools would appear. If they didn't appear, then at any moment he could look up to me and sign (he had profound loss of hearing): Apple? Car? Sticker book? Swimming? Cereal? And I would smile and go into the bag and get it. The bag was packed to facilitate the day. He would have everything he needed to accomplish the journey of the day and the tasks we had to achieve.

Our personality, skills and spiritual gifts are similar to the items in my son's day bag. God gives them to us. When we get them is not really relevant; the important thing is that we have them to accomplish the journey of the day and the tasks before us.

It would be very frustrating for my child to rip open his bag at the beginning of the day and see swimming shorts, toy cars, a present with indecipherable writing, my wallet, my phone, his sticker book, my iPad, a bag of cereal, a towel, two nappies, my notepad and his headphones. He could guess some of the events of the day, but about others he would have no idea, and he certainly wouldn't know the order of events.

So often we do that with our spiritual gifts! We stare at our individual make-up to try and find out what the journey of our life will be, and what great things we should accomplish. We rummage around in our spiritual day bag and try to solve the mystery of our purpose by analysing the contents.

We often do this to ourselves and to our children. We try to figure out our gifts. We analyse ourselves and our children. We take the quiz.

It is a frustrating place to be for two reasons: 1) spiritual gifts are not designed to forecast our future, just to facilitate it, and 2) we could be wrong in our assessment of ourselves or we could limit ourselves. God designed us. He knows all he put into us already, and he will continue to give us what we need as we go along (1 Corinthians 12:4–7). If we decide what gifts we have and don't have, we may miss what God is prompting us to do because we have already judged our lack of suitability instead of confidently moving in the opportunities God has created for us.

I take my child to the leisure centre for the purpose of swimming: to enjoy himself, to learn how to swim and to meet with friends. I pack the bag with everything he needs to participate fully. I go with him into the pool. If my child refused to go into the leisure centre because he didn't see the swimming shorts in his bag, it would be ridiculous. He goes into the leisure centre full of excitement because we are together and I have taken him there. He doesn't even think about whether or not I have what he needs.

Often we are more like Moses. He had been raised in Pharaoh's household, and his character had been shaped by God. God drew Moses to a place to talk with him about the next step.

The Lord said, 'I have indeed seen the misery of my people in Egypt. I have heard them crying out because of their slave drivers, and I am concerned about their suffering. So I have come down to rescue them from the hand of the Egyptians and to bring them up out of that land into a good and spacious land, a land flowing with milk and honey—the home of the Canaanites, Hittites, Amorites, Perizzites, Hivites and Jebusites. And now the cry of the Israelites has reached me, and I have seen the way the Egyptians are oppressing them. So now, go. I am sending you to Pharaoh to bring my people the Israelites out of Egypt.'

But Moses said to God, 'Who am I that I should go to Pharaoh and bring the Israelites out of Egypt?' (Exodus 3:7–11)

This is a very understandable question to ask. It is probably one I would ask as well. This is a huge and terrifying undertaking, and Moses seeks some sort of affirmation of identity, some sort of assurance of his ability to accomplish what God is asking him to do. So how does God respond?

And God said, 'I will be with you. And this will be the sign to you that it is I who have sent you: When you have brought the people out of Egypt, you will worship God on this mountain.' (v. 12)

I find it fascinating that God didn't respond with, 'I have given you the skills and gifts to be able to do this. You are perfect just the way you are.' Instead, he said, 'I will be with you.'

Moses asked more questions about how it would work, and God promised miracles and riches for his people and a guarantee of God's fulfilled purpose. But Moses wasn't done. He spotted a flaw in God's great plan: his own personality and gifts.

Moses said to the Lord, 'Pardon your servant, Lord. I have never been eloquent, neither in the past nor since you have spoken to your servant. I am slow of speech and tongue.'

The Lord said to him, 'Who gave human beings their mouths? Who makes them deaf or mute? Who gives them sight or makes them blind? Is it not I, the Lord? Now go; I will help you speak and will teach you what to say.' But Moses said, 'Pardon your servant, Lord. Please send someone else.' (4:10–13)

You see, even after seeing those miracles in front of him, Moses still didn't believe that God could use him. He trusted in what he could see over what God had planned and provided. God simply asked Moses to trust that the 'day bag' he would provide would have everything he needed, but Moses wasn't able to do so. He tried to bail out of the whole calling, refusing God because of his own judgment of what he was capable of doing.

Gideon had a similar experience. God came to him to draw him into the exciting task of defending his people from severe oppression.

'Pardon me, my lord,' Gideon replied, 'but how can I save Israel? My clan is the weakest in Manasseh, and I am the least in my family.'

The Lord answered, 'I will be with you, and you will strike down all the Midianites, leaving none alive.' (Judges 6:15–16)

I love how Gideon even details how ridiculous he is. I do this often to God: list my terribleness, waiting for his affirmation to rush into my insecurity and to confirm to me why I am the perfect person for this. But God doesn't respond by convincing Gideon of his suitability. Later, we learn that God's whole approach to saving Israel was to keep them as weak as possible so that they would see God more clearly. When Gideon responded to his call with fear and seeking affirmation, God replied by declaring his presence and power.

Over and over, it is God's presence and power that makes the difference. God drew Moses and Gideon closer into relationship to facilitate their purposes. Our children need to take more comfort and confidence from God's presence than from their belief in themselves.

When Samuel was choosing David to be the new king, he said, 'People look at the outward appearance, but the Lord looks at the heart' (1 Samuel 16:7). We will never see the way God sees. We all have strengths and weaknesses and spiritual gifts, but God's evaluation of what those things are and how he chooses to use them are his alone. He may ask us to operate out of what we see as weaknesses because it puts us in a place of spiritual and emotional vulnerability to his guidance. Or he may call us to a place where we discover strengths we never knew we had. When we over-focus on trying to define and know ourselves for the sake of knowing our purpose, we limit our trust in the Creator who calls us to that purpose.

Children are used to this idea of destiny: this end point towards which we are headed. Our stories are full of it. Romances end at the wedding. Movie hero stories end at the success of the task or the full embracing of a hero's identity. You figure out who you are and then you act on it, or you focus on the task you are set to accomplish and you succeed. Our children have responded most often in either one of two ways: 1) that they are not a hero or someone extraordinary, and so aspire only to live a fairly ordinary, mundane life: get a job, have a family, and live; or 2) that God has a specific and significant thing he wants them to do, and they have to work hard to find it and accomplish it, like a secret agent—neither of which is true.

If you look at hero stories in the Bible, a life calling really was a series of relationship-based decisions in response to God's voice. We can see the whole arc of the story, but for the main hero at the time, it was one step in front of the other, living out her purposefulness in God's story the best she could each day.

I think our desperate desire to *know* is a fairly modern concept. We want to know where we are headed. We want to know the end point before we begin. We want to line up our life and be in control of its steps. In some ways, we want to know what the big calling of our life is so that we can take control and plot how to achieve it. We want our assignment so that we can get on with doing it. I think, more often than not, God says, 'Follow me' and promises his guidance and clear voice. As we follow, our unique purpose and path unfolds before us.

When we look at how Jesus led his disciples on their life journeys, there was no one way. Most of the time, he said simply, 'Follow me.' He told a few that they would be fishers of people (Matthew 4:18–20), but to others he simply extended an invitation (see, for example, Matthew 9:9). He didn't say, 'Bartholomew, follow me and you will be the admin guy for this ministry for three years, and then grow in your business career in Jerusalem after I've gone, and then switch it for a life as a tanner later in life to please your wife and because you like working with your hands.' He simply said, 'Follow me.'

The promises from God about the direction of our lives aren't that he will supernaturally appear or give us a 'sign' every time we have a decision to make. He promises simply to lead us in the ordinary, everyday way. 'If you go the wrong way—to the right or to the left—you will hear a voice behind you saying, "This is the right way. You should go this way" ' (Isaiah 30:21, NCV). 'But when he, the Spirit of truth, comes, he will guide you into all the truth. He will not speak on his own; he will speak only what he hears, and he will tell you what is yet to come' (John 16:13, NIV).

My prayer for my child is not that he will accomplish one great big thing, but that he will live in relationship with God each day, impacting others and living his place in God's greater story.

The purpose of our lives isn't to find the career that is right or the one big thing God is asking us to do. Our purpose is to love God with all our heart, soul, mind and strength, and love our neighbour as ourselves. We are to flourish in relationship with God and partner with him to transform one life at a time in love, one situation at a time. Sometimes the task looks huge, and sometimes it looks small, but it is always, always, significant.

This is why our children have a purpose from birth. They are capable of being significant always, capable of transforming moments always, capable of walking in relationship with God and following him in the world always.

Our journeys of purpose are often much more winding and erratic than we instinctively think they should be. We have a fantasy that one day we will wake up and know our one big calling in life and then pursue it relentlessly until it is accomplished. I don't know where we got that idea, because as we look around, there is virtually no one who does that! Look at the people in the Bible. Look at your friends. Look at your own journey.

In the end, our unique, individual life path is just a series of decisions to live the purposes God has called us to each day. Some days, this will include big, life-altering decisions, and other days, it will include ministering peace to a small child. The process is the same. Each day we wake up determined to love God and love others, responding to needs and opportunities in relationship with him, and it is up to God to guide us. Moses didn't know his entire future at the beginning, but at the end of his days he could look back across his life and see the grand path that he was on, and one day our children will too.

As parents, our job is to prepare our children not for the one big thing that they will do or the career they will have. Our children are constantly changing and adapting, adding skills and growing in their sensitivities and character. Any time we look at our children, we see only a snapshot, one moment in their life's journey. Our job is not to build a path around that single snapshot, but to prepare our children to live their daily purpose in better and better relationship with God and to empower them to follow him wherever he is asking them to go. The next two chapters will explore some practical ways we can position our children to respond to the daily opportunities of calling that each of us is given.

— Chapter 8 —

Shaping our response

'MUMMYYYYYY!' The tiny one-year-old screamed as she saw her mother leave the crèche room for the main service. Her little body shuffled towards the door and she pressed herself up against it, straining for the door handle.

Other children ignored her agony and played with the array of toys scattered about as a crèche leader attempted to distract her and draw her into the play area, to no avail.

Eli, aged two, stood frozen, looking at the distraught girl. 'Lost. Sad. Oh no!' he exclaimed and glanced up at me. 'That's right, Eli. She is feeling lost and sad. What can we do to help her feel happy?' He tentatively approached the sobbing child and wrapped his arms around her. She paused in her screaming, then turned to him and pleaded, 'Mummy!' The tears returned.

'Idea! Toy!' said Eli. He ran over to the toys and grabbed his favourite one, returning to the girl, car extended. 'Look! Car! Happy, go fast! Brrmmmm brrmmmmmm.' The girl froze in surprise, tears flowing, and looked in confusion at this small person waving a car in front of her. She took the car and then shuffled close to him. Eli hugged her and patted her head gently. 'Happy. All right! Sit,' he said quietly. He sat down and started playing with the toys, and she sat down next to him, their sides touching. Her breathing slowed. 'All right. Safe.' Eli said. He patted her leg, repeating the words.

'Look! She happy! All better.' His face beamed with pride. 'I did it! Nice and happy.' He patted her again and they played together.

Purpose is part of our birthright. It is part of the make-up of who we are. We have been created with a call to be purposeful, both now and in the future, and we can position our children to be ready to respond to the daily calls of purpose that God lays in front of them.

One life matters

One of the most important ideas we can impress upon our children is that one life matters. The difference we can make in the life of one individual is remarkable and worthwhile. The world tells children that success is about the big and the many; that helping thousands of people at one time is much better than helping just one; that running a big fundraiser is more important than giving your pocket money away; that big impressive purpose is more important than hidden yet significant purpose.

Thinking that 'big' purpose is better than 'small' can trap our children into believing that they must strive to impact multitudes to be purposeful, when the reality is that every life matters. Every individual is cherished by God, and every day we can bring significant and real blessing and love to someone who is hurting. That is the work of Jesus. He healed people one by one when he met them, face to face. He eased emotional brokenness one person at a time. He died for humankind, but he came to earth to meet and minister to the individual. When we begin to raise the profile of ministering to individuals, a life of purpose becomes possible and significant. I would be happy if my child worked in a low-status job his whole life but loved God with his whole heart and daily transformed lives around him.

This is where the whole story of the gospel is essential. When we seed into our children the whole story of a broken world and Jesus' desire and power to restore and reconnect, then they can see that pattern in people's lives around them. The shepherd went after one lost sheep. God went after his lost people. And Eli went after one lost toddler in the crèche. Each life matters. Each day of purpose matters.

The character to do it well

Character is something that we are growing in our children already. It's the job of every parent. Each one of us is already trying to grow humble, loving, strong children who love God and act respectfully and kindly. It is helpful to remember that character matters for spiritual purpose as well as for daily life in the world.

A key aspect of parenting for our children's specific purpose is to focus our parenting on growing our children's characters, so that they are able to fulfil the opportunities that God has for them. In the Old Testament, both Moses and Joseph were taken on a journey of character refinement before they were able and ready to take the big step to a greater level of influence.

Look at Moses when he lived in Pharaoh's palace. He was compassionate, quick to anger, rash and impulsive. One day he saw an Egyptian beating a Hebrew. He looked around, thought that no one was looking, and then killed the Egyptian and buried him in the sand (see Exodus 2:11–12). Didn't regret it one bit. Impulse to defend the weak and powerless? Fantastic. Character that solved the problem by deliberate murder? Needed some work. At that point, this man was not ready to lead the Hebrews out of Egypt with wisdom, humility, grace, and holiness. God needed to refine his character to make him ready for a future season of daily purpose.

As our children's character grows, so will their ability to bear larger roles as they live out their daily purpose. That doesn't negate their current usefulness to God. Each season of purpose is precious and effective. It simply means that as they grow and as their character strengthens, so will their ability to step into more influential or complex opportunities. Our goal is to cultivate a character that will be able to respond humbly to whatever God-opportunities may arise, small and large.

Some of the most unsung heroes in the Bible are the parents of the people whose stories we know. The parents grew in their children a sense of purposefulness and the strength of character to be ready for God's prompting and calling.

I wish I knew what Mary and Joseph's parents were like. Think of it! They managed to grow children who as teenagers loved God enough and had the cultivated character to respond faithfully to God's calling to bear scorn and shame and to raise the child of the living God. The decisions Mary and Joseph made were just the next steps in a series of purpose-filled decisions they had made up until that moment.

We can't predict what our children's paths on earth will be but we can prepare our children. God will lead them through their journey.

Responding to their developing sensitivity

Throughout our children's lives, and as their personalities and characters develop, their hearts will resonate with particular topics, and personal interests will emerge. Our goal is to facilitate the growth of their souls as they encounter new experiences and new situations. God is also developing your children, and the opportunities of purpose he will create for them now and in the future will draw together their life experiences and interests.

For instance, my child is currently particularly sensitive to people who are feeling pain. When he is watching television, the thing that most disturbs him is people getting yelled at or falling down. He was profoundly hard of hearing for half his life, so he is very tuned into faces and emotions. When he is around adults, teens or children that I know to be fragile or having a hard time in life, I see him behave differently. Normally a boisterous child, he is very gentle around them and often will lightly touch their knees or shoulders or pat reassuringly. In most games that he plays, he will create accident scenarios and spend the majority of the play time rescuing and comforting the vehicles and stuffed animals involved in the extensive and traumatic accident. If there is a child crying in a room, Caleb will inevitably walk over to the child and try to help or sit next to him to give him some companionship while he is sad. When he is playing and another child grabs his toy, he will grab it back, but if the other child is upset about it, Caleb will instinctively share (or hide the toy and come back to comfort). Emotion currently trumps possessions with him.

Will this sensitivity continue for his whole life? I don't know. I do know that it is of particular importance to him now, so I am doing all I can to facilitate him growing in and learning skills based on this sensitivity. As it becomes part of his character, I want to do all I can to help it settle into his mind and spirit in a way that honours God. If this sensitivity were left undiscipled, he could learn to be powerless in the face of others' pain or to be afraid of it. I prefer to train him to respond with compassion and strength, to frame for him what God is doing in response to other people's pain, and to offer him opportunities to learn how to respond in those circumstances.

Who knows? Next month Caleb could be completely wrapped up in a passion for sport, and I would rejoice in that with him and help to shape his character through those circumstances as well.

Children's interests, passions and spiritual sensitivities will be constantly changing throughout their lives, and our job is to walk alongside them on their journeys, facilitating the development of characters that can bear and operate out of purpose well.

We are on a journey with our children, helping them to discover what fascinates them, what excites them, and what resonates with their personality and spiritual heart. The more we can expose our children to new situations and adventures, the more chances we have to spark their hearts and shape their characters.

Every experience in life informs our children and gives them memories to draw from and skills to use on the journey. David played the harp and God used it to minister to Saul. Moses lived in Pharaoh's palace, so he knew how to deal with the court. Peter was a fisherman, so he instinctively understood what it meant to be a fisher of people. Every part of our path can be used by God.

Children's breadth of experiences and skills helps them to understand the world, God's creation and other people better. It's OK to let our children flourish in their experiences, trusting that the God who weaves all together is shaping our children.

Keeping connected to God

In order for our children to live their purpose, they need to be God-connected. In the Bible, we see that God's promises to people were about his presence, his closeness and companionship and the power that comes with that. In fact, the promise God repeats most often in the Bible is 'I will be with you.'

Our children deserve to live in a two-way relationship with God, sharing their hearts, hearing his voice, knowing his touch in response. Purpose flows out of relationship, so it is essential that we help our children connect themselves to God in order to do confidently what he is inviting them to do in this world. Why not try highlighting God's presence and how to have a relationship with him, using the six-stage circle? If you want to explore this more, then *Parenting Children for a Life of Faith* is a book that will help you.

Spiritual gifts

Being connected to God isn't the only spiritual component to purpose. Scripture lists many spiritual gifts: serving, teaching, prophecy, faith, exhortation, giving, leadership, mercy, words of wisdom, words of knowledge, faith, healing, miracles, discerning between spirits, tongues and interpretation of tongues, apostleship, helping, administration, evangelism and pastoring (Romans 12:6–8; 1 Corinthians 12:8–10, 28; Ephesians 4:11; 1 Peter 4:11). Some people believe that there are more, and these are just examples the biblical authors highlighted, while others believe that this is the complete list. The purpose of these gifts is for the good of others

(1 Corinthians 12:4–7). They are given to us to help us minister to others, not to give us identity and better self-knowledge.

We can often be confused about how much emphasis to place on spiritual gifts with our children. I would suggest that we don't give our children quizzes to help them find their gifts or show them lists of all the gifts that are out there. I think that it is important to remember that these gifts are not the end point but a facilitation of our purpose.

It can be helpful to discuss the idea of spiritual gifts with them, and how God's tools for changing people's lives are amazing and come from him. We can chat about how when God asks us to do things, he will equip us to do it, and that these gifts are a part of our equipping. If he wants us to use a gift, we will feel that it is right at the time. We can assure our children that our spiritual day bags will always contain what is needed for us to do what God is asking us to do.

Our children are growing and flexing and developing, and while we can see trends in their lives, it is most helpful to allow them the flexibility to grow into their uniqueness without the need to quantify and define it.

Spiritual gifts help them to live every day well, equipping them to be significant in the relationships, places and areas of influence that they are in. We can tell our children that the gifts exist and that they are to help them love powerfully in the places that touch their hearts.

We can tell them that God will lead, equip and help them to accomplish any task into which he draws them. We can also tell them that spiritual gifts are not to be focused on or planned from. They are powerful, equipping gifts that God freely gives us to live purposefully every day and to accomplish what he has set before us.

The six-stage circle

So how do we invest in our children so that they have a purposeful and unique journey, walking every day together with God? Here are a few practical suggestions for how to begin to explore these ideas with your children:

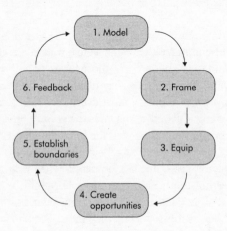

Model

Give your children a peek into your motivations when you do things. Modelling counts, whether it's small or large. My husband told my son this week, 'Mummy is feeling very tired and stressed, and so I'm cleaning the house because it helps her to feel loved and happy and not worried.' All week, my child has randomly jumped off the couch and picked something up off the floor and put it away, saying, 'Love Mummy.'

Tell your child when something hits your current sensitivity and how you are responding to it. 'Lately, whenever I see a young teenage mum on our bus, my heart beats fast and I feel as if my stomach flips upside down. I just keep thinking about how important having friends and family to help me was when you and your brother were small, and how she may not have that. I don't know why my heart is so sensitive to people in her situation right now, but I definitely want to do something about it. I just feel that God's poking my heart about it, so I'm going to have a think about what to do next.'

Frame

Watching your children play is often a great way to get a feel for their sensitivities and to be able to frame those for them. In fantasy games, what is the plot? What role do they play? My child is all about the rescue. For over a year now, almost every game involves someone getting lost or stuck. He then becomes the rescuer, coming in to lift the car back on to the table, fixing the helicopter wings or opening the door for me when I'm 'stuck' in the bathroom. He doesn't want to fight bad guys, just rescue people who have accidents. I find it interesting that of all the scripts he could be playing out in his head, this is the one he loves doing right now. What does your children's play look like? Are they the policeman who protects everyone else? Or the host who welcomes in? Or the teacher who leads when you play school? Whatever it is, while they are playing, try framing how what they are doing is a powerful example of the purpose that God has for us and is part of God's story. To my child, who loves rescuing, I read the Bible story of the lost sheep and tell him how Jesus was sent to rescue all of us from our sin. To a child whose current sensitivity and play is about protecting people, you could read Bible stories about Gideon and Hezekiah and how they partnered with God to defend people. You could also tell stories of times when your child protected people, and how that is spiritually and physically important and part of what God asks us to do on earth. No matter what your child's current sensitivity or interest is, you can surround it with scriptural backing and practical everyday stories so that they can see how important it is to God and others.

Watch movies or television together, with the particular view of seeing how important character is to what the main person accomplishes in the story. If you are doing this with younger children, just watch and comment out loud, naming what you see. 'Doc McStuffins is so kind. She stops her whole day just to help heal one stuffed animal. Just like Jesus! Wow, she does help a lot!' For older children you can wonder together about what could have been: 'What would have happened if the main person let it all go to her head and thought she was better than other people? Do you think she would have done things differently? Do you think she would have been as effective in accomplishing her task?' You can also look at the bad guy in the show and ask, 'What makes him so different from the good guy?' Often the 'bad guy' has a character flaw, rather than being 'evil'.

Equip

Celebrate failure. Often in a grand failure there are a thousand tiny victories of character and achievement. Take your ten-year-old out for an ice cream for showing grace and honour in the face of losing a race (instead of to try to make him feel better for losing). I have a friend who has a particular value for seeing every situation as a chance to improve. She inspires her children to think that way too. When her six-year-old comes off the court after losing a tennis match, he flings his hands in the air with a big smile and yells, 'Hey, Mum, I'm *learning*!'

Give your children possible ways to respond to what is in their heart. If your child seems to have sensitivity for generosity and helping lift people's sadness, then feed that. Show your child television shows where people are overwhelmed with generosity, or video testimonies of God using people to bless someone with the generosity of a gift, financial or otherwise. I once told my youth group a story of how, when I was much poorer than I am now, some of the youth from our church used to spend their pocket money to buy my family food and leave it on our front door and run away. I shared how blessed we were by that gift and how much it helped us. The next week some of the children were buzzing. Children who really had a passion for helping people in need with generosity came back to church giggling with stories of giving away toys, spending pocket money on a sandwich for a homeless man (with parental permission and supervision) and buying a new pen for their dad when his broke. A new pattern emerged in those specific children because their passion was fed with testimonies of the power of that sensitivity put into action.

Create opportunities

Expand your child's experiences of the world in order to open their eyes and hearts to new areas of sensitivity. Visit the children's ward at a local hospital and play with the children there. Volunteer to clean a homeless shelter. Read the *National Geographic* magazine together and discuss places around the world and what people's lives are like. Visit a church that is a different denomination to yours, and highlight the similarities of how people love God and how they express it in a different way. Take your child to an evening where a missionary is sharing about her work.

When you are out together and see something that spiritually stirs you, point it out to your children and tell them what is going on in your heart. Invite them to chat with God about it in their heads, just sharing what they are thinking and feeling.

Invite your children to minister in your family. So often we want to rush to release children into leadership in the world or in our church, but actually your family is a great place to begin. I would consider your family a key place to release your children's purpose and passions. Whatever sensitivities are being raised in your children, invite them to use those in your family. If they have a particular heart for art, ask them to paint a Bible verse picture for your hallway. If they have a sensitivity to people who are hurting physically, ask them to be the ones to get the first aid kit and help dress wounds, or to turn off lights and get your pillows when you have a headache. When you release your family to minister, you can train them how to view themselves and their usefulness in the world.

Establish boundaries

Be aware of your child's character development as well as their behaviour. When I was a child, I was involved in theatre. This particular company would go out after the performance to meet the audience and sign autographs (for some reason, children loved getting these). I was ten, and while my behaviour towards people was absolutely fine, there was something sneaking into my character, a superiority and pride, that my mother was not about to let stand. She sat me down and talked to me about my attitude and about the value of other people. I was told that my character was more important to her than my opportunities, and if I couldn't figure out how to bless other people and keep an appropriate view of myself, then I wasn't going to be allowed to go outside and sign autographs. She knew that no matter what God used me for, I couldn't afford to have arrogance or pride as part of my character.

Feedback

Focus on character as well as accomplishments. When your children do something, praise the character they showed as well as acknowledging what they achieved. 'Well done! That violin recital was fantastic! Beautiful! I have to say my favourite part, though, was when you were all walking on to the stage and the boy in front of you tripped. All the other children kept walking and some even laughed, but you helped him up, brushed him off and helped him pick up his music. You knew he would be embarrassed, and so you helped him. My heart just wanted to explode. I was so proud of you!'

Debrief with children particular moments when they touched one life well and how God equipped them to do it, even without their noticing. One dad I knew had this exchange with his nine-year-old son: 'I noticed how that girl got left behind by her other friends and you walked over. I expected that you would invite her to play, but you just sat next to her and read a book! She read over your shoulder for a while, and then you started talking. She seemed to feel so happy and not lonely anymore. How did you know that reading a book was the best way to help?' 'I don't know,' he said. 'I was going to ask her to play, but then I just felt that would be wrong. I just felt that reading a book would make her feel less stressed.' The dad smiled. 'You know, buddy, I think that God gave you that knowledge, so you could help that girl in the best way possible. Pretty cool that you did just what God was asking you to do, and he helped you do it by telling you something you couldn't have known.'

*

— Chapter 9 —

Poised to act

Ruth had determined that she was needed. There was a need in front of her, a big gaping hole that required filling, and she figured she could sort it out. She was seven. On a Sunday morning, the crèche set-up and take-down was laborious, and the adult leaders struggled to get it all done in time. She asked permission to take charge of it. Our leaders agreed, and Ruth leapt into action. On time every Sunday, she would show up and work with passion and excellence to get everything out and set up just right. After church, she press-ganged her friends into helping with take-down, delaying the post-church playing until it was all finished. Week in and week out, this seven-year-old girl led a team of five or six children in the set-up and take-down of the crèche, not because she was shoved there because of her age, or because it was the simplest task adults could think to give her, but because she saw a need and decided to use her power to change the situation. She wasn't a helper or an add-on. She was essential to the process of a Sunday morning, and she was counted on. Her ministry brought real blessing, not just a tolerant smile.

The inevitable outworking of purpose is action. When we love God and love others, our actions flow out of that genuine place of love, and we want to respond with action. This is why it is so important that we lay the spiritual, mental and emotional foundations of our children well, so that their daily lives, choices and actions will reflect an inner life of love and strength.

It can be a common mistake for us as parents so to want our children to live purposeful lives that we accidentally push them into doing good works. While doing good works may be a good trait to build in our children, it does not foster and grow children's faith or create a lasting and permanent sense of spiritual purpose. James, a disciple of Jesus, insisted that faith without deeds is useless, but that when faith and actions are working together, faith is made complete by the actions (James 2:14–26). So as we talk about how to encourage and equip children's actions of purpose, it is essential that we approach it with a view to cultivating the desires and actions that flow from the heart, and not from a position of how we can encourage children to do good things. We cannot stop at cultivating their spiritual centres; we also have the joy of discipling and empowering our children's acts of love and purpose.

When our children are poised to be proactively purposeful throughout the day, then we have the honour of empowering their responses to what their hearts are provoked by, and to God's prompting of direction.

In order to do this well, we as parents must position ourselves to empower and coach our children, rather than partner with them or drive the action. We must treat them as powerful people who are genuinely responding from a heart of purpose. If we can manage not to insert ourselves into the centre of our children's actions, then we ensure that their journey of purpose stays theirs. They will be able to own the fruit they will see, the achievements they will make, the connection to God and others they will experience, and the life lessons they will learn. By allowing them to be the motivators, inventors and main workers, we allow their character to be forged and enable them to learn how to respond to the joys and difficulties of purpose. I would rather a child raised £30 on his own than £500 because his parent jumped on board and made it happen. Our job in all of this is to cheer them on and facilitate them practically, spiritually and emotionally. We can help them see the changes they make in individual lives, their communities and the world.

Coaching their hearts' response

As our children go through life, they will naturally run across experiences that provoke their hearts or push on their current sensitivities. When we train our children to see power when they look in the mirror, they will begin to feel more and more confident to act when they run across something that disturbs them or plays on their mind.

When I was a child, I became paralysed in almost all situations that required physical response. I would knock a glass of milk over and my mother would leap up, but for me the world slowed down. I would watch the cup start to fall over, then hit the table and spill. I would sit perfectly still and watch the milk flow off the table and the glass roll off, smashing on the ground. I would sit and watch in shock, my mind completely blank. Then, inevitably, my mother, who by now had found a cloth and was sorting it out, would look up at me and say (in a blend of patience and exasperation), 'Don't just sit there. *Do* something. Move!'

I am happy to say that I am now super-fast at responding even before the scenario has fully played out—but this took some years of training, working against my natural reaction. I think many of our children share a similar response to spiritual opportunities that happen right in front of them. They are surprised by a need—a child crying, a sibling fight, a grandfather in pain, a famine in West Africa, a friend at school who is poor, or a special needs family at church—and they freeze, letting the opportunity go by; not for lack of willingness as often their hearts will feel compassion, but for lack of readiness to act.

There is a fantastic children's movie called *Robots*, in which one of the main characters is an inventor. He describes the process of inventing like this: 'So look around for a need, and start coming up with ideas to fill that need. One idea will lead to another and before you know it, you've done it. See a need. Fill a need.'

It is important for our children to know that sometimes a

need appears in front of us and we have the ability to respond. Our foundational purpose is to love, and sometimes it's our job to respond to a need when it arises. Daily purpose is sometimes simply a process of seeing a need and filling it.

A much beloved children's television host in America, Mr Rodgers, described how he learned how to view the news. 'When I was a boy and I would see scary things in the news, my mother would say, "Look for the helpers. You will always find people who are helping."' These people didn't necessarily feel 'called' to help; they responded, and that is just as powerful. Some of the greatest stories in the Bible are of people responding to a need.

Peter and John were walking to the temple when a beggar interrupted them to ask for money. Seeing his need, they responded, healing him instantly (see Acts 3).

Nehemiah heard the news of the terrible state of his homeland, and his heart responded. He instantly wept and spent days praying and seeking God. He then determined to do something about it and approached the king for permission to act (see Nehemiah 1—2).

Abigail was a woman married to an unwise man who made a potentially catastrophic mistake. As soon as she heard about it, she reacted quickly, running into the fray and acting with so much love, wisdom and bravery that she was able to turn the hearts of a leader and his army on their way to bringing destruction to her people (see 1 Samuel 25:14–35).

A heart ready to respond is a heart that can live a courageous daily life of purpose.

Planned action

Through children's regular daily chatter, we tend to learn about what is going on with them spiritually. They tell stories of what happened at school, at playgroup, in their clubs or at church. They wonder about it while watching television, or they ask questions when they are reading books. It will come up as a topic of conversation in the car or while you are making dinner. As they share about life, you will begin to notice patterns of what is stirring your children's hearts.

Most parents I know have found that the most helpful way of encouraging their children to act when their hearts and sensitivities are being stirred is to listen carefully and ask questions about the situation to help them fully explore the issue. Parents then ask the simple question, 'What are you going to do about it?' This question communicates to all children that as parents we care, that we hear them, and that we believe they can do something about the situation. We can always follow it up with an offer of support if and when they feel it's right to do something.

Sarah spent a lot of time thinking about missionaries and how lonely and homesick they could become. She read missionary stories online and talked about them frequently. When an opportunity at school arose to create a project to help someone overseas, Sarah's discussions about missionaries increased. Her mother asked the question, 'What are you going to do about it?' Sarah decided that she wanted to send boxes of familiar food, toys and books to a missionary who was teaching English as a second language in China. After submitting her idea and leading the project, over 90 kilos of 'home' were sent to this man in China. The missionary was overwhelmed and was also able to host many 'English' parties at his house, opening up opportunities for the gospel to be shared with his students much more frequently.

Raj was furious that there was a group of boys at school who would physically intimidate the younger children. They wouldn't hurt them or yell at them, but just set out to scare them every day with their presence and attitude. Raj felt intensely that it was unjust that people should be allowed to create such fear in others, especially in those so small. Raj's dad listened carefully and then asked him, 'What are you going to do about it?' Raj decided that every day he would watch the group of boys on the playground. If they started to intimidate the small ones, he would stop whatever he was doing and move over to the younger children's game so that they weren't frightened off the equipment or made to feel vulnerable. He did this for a full year, and eventually all his friends came round to the idea and joined him. The need to enforce this evaporated after one year because he so influenced the playground culture that it didn't happen anymore.

As children get into the pattern of responding to situations that press on their hearts, they will begin to internalise the process of asking themselves, 'What am I going to do about it?'

Keenan's family drove a neighbour's family to church each Sunday. This family had a son, Richard, who was a little younger than Keenan and had Down's Syndrome. The church loved Richard but struggled to know how to help him when the children were in their groups. Keenan had been building a deeper and deeper heart connection with God and began to want others to have one as well. He attended our New Wine Kids' Leadership Academy event during the summer. As he signed up, he wrote on the back of his form a suggestion that 'special needs' was a seminar we should put on for children to learn how to help children with additional needs connect with God. We were so struck by the suggestion that we hunted him down and had a chat with him. Out of the 650 forms, he was the only one who had written down 'special needs'. He told us the story of Richard, and when we asked if he would like us to put something on especially for him, he paused and then said yes. When I asked him why he paused, he smiled a bit and said, 'I wouldn't say that I'm really interested in helping people with special needs, but I am interested in helping Richard. No one else is, and I think he needs to know how to connect with God because it's awesome. So I'll do it.' We trained him up during the week and sent him back home equipped to help Richard. The following year we remembered Keenan, and so we made a special needs seminar available for children who had a heart passion or sensitivity for helping people with special needs connect with God—and 85 children signed up.

Prayer is a practical response

Sometimes we forget that prayer is also a practical action response to our children's hearts being stirred or their sensitivities being provoked. Being poised to act is not just being ready to do physical things to help, but also being ready to respond emotionally and spiritually, taking the situation to God in prayer and intercession. Prayer is potent, but often our children don't understand the potential of it. As we cultivate our children's hearts for love and action, it is helpful to give them the strength that comes from understanding how prayer can affect the world in partnership with God.

The Bible is clear about how powerful prayer is. God moves in response to our prayers, and in prayer we ourselves are transformed. We aren't meant to be carrying burdens of the heart alone. Children need to know that our loving God responds to our human desires.

James declares, 'The prayer of a righteous person is powerful and effective. Elijah was a human being, even as we are. He prayed earnestly that it would not rain, and it did not rain on the land for three and a half years. Again he prayed, and the heavens gave rain, and the earth produced its crops' (James 5:16–18).

Children can know that there is nothing too small or too large for God's attention, and it is our privilege to pray anytime, anywhere, about anything that is being stirred in our hearts.

Paul's letter to the Ephesians encourages us to 'pray in the Spirit on all occasions with all kinds of prayers and requests. With this in mind, be alert and always keep on praying for all the Lord's people' (Ephesians 6:18).

Our children can establish a pattern of bringing concerns to God in a way that brings peace and connection with the Father whose heart shares their same concerns. Paul's letter to the Philippians lays this out: 'Do not be anxious about anything, but in every situation, by prayer and petition, with thanksgiving, present your requests to God. And the peace of God, which transcends all understanding, will guard your hearts and your minds in Christ Jesus' (Philippians 4:6–7).

When our children grasp this, they begin to feel the importance of prayer as an action. One afternoon at a camp, a children's leader approached us looking upset and told us that his sister had just been taken to hospital for an abscess on her ovary. She was in such extreme pain that the maximum dosage of morphine was not working. The doctors were taking her into surgery the next day, and she was likely to lose her last ovary in the operation and, therefore, her ability to have children.

The next day, the day of the operation, nine children came to the prayer tent to pray for their leader, as they were concerned about him and his sister. These boys, between the ages of seven and ten, sat with their leader, thanked God for who he was, and asked him for his healing and peace to come on the leader's sister. The next day we got news. At the same time as the boys had been praying, the sister's pain instantly stopped. The doctors were so surprised that they did another scan. The abscess had completely disappeared, and all dead tissue had been restored. Surgery was cancelled and she was discharged. The doctors acknowledged that it was a miracle.

The children were ecstatic, as well as the leader. They prayed for other things over the next couple of days. Sometimes they saw the fulfilment of their prayers, other times they didn't. But they kept praying.

Prayer is powerful, and we are told that prayer is key to our purpose on earth. If we truly love people, we will naturally want to bring them and their situations to our Father God. It is our job not only to empower our children to act physically in response to their hearts, but also to react spiritually. If we focus on cultivating their hearts, then the big question of whether or not we see our requests fulfilled is less important than the genuine heart response of living in connection with God and bringing our requests to him.

Empowering God-directed opportunities

We can go through life completely focused on ourselves and on what we need to accomplish in the day. I'm always struck by the oddity of it when I'm on a train. Here we all are, crammed into a tin can speeding down a track centimetres away from each other, yet we are all trying to exist in our own little worlds. We prize having that privacy, that space. It is so easy to switch that isolation on as we walk down the road, go shopping, sit in church or while we are working. That switch, though, often isolates us from God's promptings as well. Part of living out our purpose every day means lowering those barriers more and more, and making ourselves aware of what opportunities God may be opening up, what he may be whispering to our hearts, and what he may be asking us to do for people and situations around us.

For every one of us, each day is a new opportunity to live full of purpose, ready to impact the world. Our children need to know that they have a choice: to go through the day focused only on themselves, or to be aware of their own heart, of the needs of people around them and of what God may ask them to do. We can create a culture and understanding in our home so that every day we wake up and think, 'What shall we do today, God? I am ready.'

Our children need to learn what that prompting looks and feels like in everyday life. As parents, we are in the position to be able to create windows into how we hear and respond to God's promptings daily. They will watch us go through our day and look for how we respond to other people. They will notice when we stop along the road or change our plans because of something we feel pressing on our heart. We can frame for them what is happening inside us when we hear God.

I was walking in the rain with a friend's ten-year-old child, Molly. We were huddled under my umbrella, trying to walk quickly to a shop to get some drinks. We passed by a homeless man who had set up a little temporary place of warmth in a doorway. He wasn't getting wet and he looked warm enough. As soon as I walked past him, I felt a check in my heart. I felt that I needed to go back and give that man our umbrella. I fought with God and told him that this was an expensive umbrella, and that I couldn't let my friend's child get soaked. I highlighted that he'd never asked me to give away my umbrella before, and so why was now so important? After about 20 steps, God was unconvinced by my arguments, and I knew I had a choice to take the opportunity or pass it by. I turned my head around, and I repositioned my selfish heart to love this man for whom God had asked me to sacrifice so little.

'Hold on, sweetie. Stay here, I'll be right back,' I said, pulling her into a doorway and interrupting what she was telling me about her day. I dashed back in the pouring rain and offered the man my umbrella. He looked confused, and I quickly said, 'Sorry to bother you, sir, but God told me to come back and give this to you.' The man looked at me and said, 'But you're getting wet.' I smiled as water soaked through my shirt. 'I guess God was less concerned about me getting wet than about you having this! He really likes you a lot, you know.' I laughed and he laughed and I ran back to Molly. We fashioned our bags into coverings and dashed to the next coffee shop we could find.

'What was that all about?' she asked as we sat down. I told her the whole story and her eyes got wider and wider. We talked for half an hour about how God speaks, about his love for people, and why my heart got selfish. We talked about her experiences with God, and his purposes for both of us.

The more we debrief our experiences with children, the more we can ask our children about theirs. We can create the space in our errands to ensure that as we go about together, they have the opportunity to respond to what they feel God is prompting their hearts about. We can surround them with stories and opportunities to act in response to God.

God is already stirring our children's hearts, even at an early age. If we listen, we can help to shape their understanding of it quite early on. Isaac was two and ran up to Sally, his mum, during the worship at church, insisting that she leave her seat and come to the back of church to hug a woman she barely knew. Isaac's mum resisted for a while, but Isaac was so insistent that she began to think something beyond Isaac's playfulness was at work. She stood up, followed him to the back and stood quietly, watching the woman for any signs of distress or any indication that a random hug would be helpful. She didn't see any, so she started to head back to her seat, but then Isaac stamped and repeated, 'Hug the lady, please.'

Sally tiptoed up to the end of the aisle, slipped her arm around the woman and said, 'Good to see you. How are you doing?' The woman turned her head, looked at Sally and tears filled her eyes. Sally gently pulled the woman to a side room, and they talked for an hour. Sally was later able to tell Isaac how good it was that he and God asked her to hug the woman, and he glowed with pride. 'Isaac helped the lady!'

When we begin to coach our children towards responding to what provokes their hearts and sensitivities, to the needs that are in front of them and to God's prompting of direction, then we can empower our children to match their action with their hearts. We can show them how, in the process of responding, God has equipped them with his voice and his gifts. We can highlight how the power he gave them as individuals has impacted people and the world around them.

*

— Chapter 10 —

Part of the body

Two boys joined our church around the same time, and they were in the same school year. One was outgoing, and one seemed very shy. Both were going through all the insecurities of joining a new church and establishing who they were in a new community. They floated for a couple of months, and their parents and I were becoming concerned. These children had heart-to-heart connections with God; their parents had discipled them in that. They were also very confident in who they were, both in how God made them and in what that meant in the wider community. But that wasn't enough for them to feel that they belonged in our church. They needed purpose in the body of Christ.

As I came alongside these families and matched the boys up with other adults and teens in the church who saw their passions and skills, these boys began to flourish. One of the boys, Asher, loved praying and listening to God. One day as we were all worshipping, he was suddenly reminded of a verse in the Bible, a promise of God's presence in struggle. As he pondered the verse, he felt that it would be helpful to share it with the senior pastor during worship. Asher came to me, and I walked with him to the front row so that he could chat with the pastor. Our pastor listened to Asher and thought that the congregation would be encouraged by what he had to say. He asked Asher to come up to the front and share the verse with the church himself. Asher was shaking when he shared it with the congregation, but he was able to see with his own eyes how people responded to the encouragement that God shared with him. He came back to his seat glowing, and throughout the next weeks and months he grew in confidence in his connection with

God and in his usefulness to the church body. He joined the prayer team and served faithfully. He worshipped more intensely and for longer. He talked to people more before and after church. He began to call it 'our church' instead of 'the church I go to'.

It's a well-known strategy to give children 'jobs' in order to engage them in a programme. Getting children involved can indeed gain their engagement, but the change in Asher wasn't because we gave him a job. He changed because God spoke to his heart and gave him an authentic purpose in his community.

I keep coming back to Paul's analogy of how a church is like a body:

A person's body is one thing, but it has many parts. Though there are many parts to a body, all those parts make only one body. Christ is like that also. Some of us are Jews, and some are Greeks. Some of us are slaves, and some are free. [I would add in here, 'Some are adults, some are children.'] *But we were all baptised into one body through one Spirit. And we were all made to share in the one Spirit.*

The human body has many parts. The foot might say, 'Because I am not a hand, I am not part of the body.' But saying this would not stop the foot from being a part of the body. The ear might say, 'Because I am not an eye, I am not part of the body.' But saying this would not stop the ear from being a part of the body. If the whole body were an eye, it would not be able to hear. If the whole body were an ear, it would not be able to smell. If each part of the body were the same part, there would be no body. But truly God put all the parts, each one of them, in the body as he wanted them...

So then there are many parts, but only one body. The eye cannot say to the hand, 'I don't need you!' And the head cannot say to the foot, 'I don't need you!' No! Those parts of the body that seem to be the weaker are really necessary. And the parts of the body we think are less deserving are the parts to which we give the most honour. We give special respect to the parts we want to hide. The more respectable parts of our body need no special care. But God put the body together and gave more honour to the parts that need it so our body would not be divided. God wanted the different parts to care the same for each other. If one part of the body suffers, all the other parts suffer with it. Or if one part of our body is honoured, all the other parts share its honour. Together you are the body of Christ, and each one of you is a part of that body.' (1 Corinthians 12:12–18, 20–27, NCV)

Too long we have stood apart as a church and looked at children and teens and said, 'We love you, we value you, but we don't need you.' For too long children have been able to look at the adult church and say the same. Often they are so disengaged from the service and the church community that their children's group or youth group culture can function without the rest of the church. We were not designed like this. Our churches were not meant to function like this. If we continue to be fragmented, then we will never experience the joy of what was promised. Have a look in Ephesians:

So Christ himself gave the apostles, the prophets, the evangelists, the pastors and teachers, to equip his people for works of service, so that the body of Christ may be built up until we all reach unity in the faith and in the knowledge of the Son of God and become mature, attaining to the whole measure of the fullness of Christ. (Ephesians 4:11–13)

The reason we need to be a full body, empowering children and youth and adults all together, is so that we can achieve the full measure of Christ. I can't experience the fullness of life in Christ unless I'm living life alongside and ministering alongside purposeful people from all parts of the body, including children and youth, and that's really challenging to me, because I'm not. I'm trying. I think there is a greater amount of God's presence, a greater amount of the Spirit, a greater amount of power and a greater amount of worship when we begin to have each member of the body empowered.

We are called to love and serve each other and this world, so that together we can 'grow up in every way into Christ' (v. 15, NCV). Another translation says that we can have the 'whole measure of the fullness of Christ' (v. 13, NIV). In order for us to experience and achieve what is possible as a church, we need to enable our children's purposes in our communities. We can't act as if we don't need them. We can't make them nice add-ons or cheerful extras. We need to begin to empower every member of the body of Christ to be an essential member. Then we will together experience a fuller and more accurate representation of what we have been called to be here on earth: the powerful body of Christ.

We have been missing what life as a church would be like with all our members ministering. We have allowed ourselves to be cheated out of something wonderful. I feel that we have cheated our children and teens out of something wonderful too: the experience of being a powerful part of a wonderful and diverse group of people who love and minister to each other. Our churches have the power to establish a community of purpose in which all people participate. We can be the place where children feel most powerful, most seen, most discipled and most released. We can be the church that God designed.

As soon as we begin to talk about this, our minds may flood with questions and objections. 'How do we do this? What would that look that on a Sunday? Surely you aren't saying that we should give children the pulpit or heap responsibility on them? What about consideration for their age? We can't abolish our leadership guidelines to allow for immature teens when we hold adults to a higher standard, can we?' All of these are right questions to ask, and some of the answers are included in the FAQs at the end of this book. It is easy to become focused on the practicalities of freeing children to participate in churches, but before we do, it is essential that we adjust some of our approaches to this idea.

See the individual, not the age

Many of us see people in categories—it seems to be the natural way we view the world. For a long time, there have been distinct categories of people in the church: 'children', 'teens', 'adults', 'the elderly', and so on. We have treated these age groups differently, writing books about how different children are from adults and how to minister to teens most effectively. We structure our ministries to target specific age groups and, more often than not, keep them separate. We encourage leadership within the age ranges, but rarely across different ages. Paul, in Galatians, has a few things to say about the members of the body of Christ:

You were all baptised into Christ, and so you were all clothed with Christ. This means that you are all children of God through faith in Christ Jesus… In Christ, there is no difference between Jew and Greek, slave and free person, male and female. You are all the same in Christ Jesus. You belong to Christ, so you are Abraham's descendants. You will inherit all of God's blessings because of the promise God made to Abraham. (Galatians 3:26, 28–29, NCV)

What would our churches look like if we didn't view age first? What if we truly believed that we are all the same in Christ Jesus? How would it be different? You see, I think that we have allowed generalisations to creep into our mindsets and rob our children and teens of their individuality. I hear people talk endlessly about what works with 'children' and how 'teens' respond. Debates arise around allowing 'children' to serve or 'teens' to lead teams. We can so easily get sucked into judging a group of people by our generalisations. I don't think we need a revolution in thinking. I think we need a relaxation of thought, a letting go of our strict categories.

We stereotype children so much. We can all think of some of these stereotypes. Children need fun programmes to learn. Children have a purer spirituality. Teens are irresponsible leaders but good helpers. Children and teens find church boring. Children have a 'simple faith'. Teens need a 'cool' factor. I believe that we treat 'children' and 'teens' as blocks of uniform people. No wonder it gets difficult when we think about releasing them into ministry in our churches and communities.

If we stop thinking in generalities, if we stop thinking of 'children' and 'youth', and instead look at Alice, Samuel and Callum, then most of our stress and debates go away. Should 'children' be allowed to be on the welcome team? I don't know, but I do know that eight-year-old Olga has a heart for the lost and lonely, and she is faithfully there at the beginning of church asking if she can help. Should 'teens' preach? I don't know, but 13-year-old Zeke has a heart for sharing scripture, and his mentor Tam thinks that he could really challenge and encourage the congregation. Can 'children' lead children younger than themselves? I don't know, but five-year-old Billy is extraordinarily kind and gentle after church with the toddlers. When one fell over after church, he not only picked him up, but prayed for him as well. When we stop thinking about 'children' and 'teens', we can begin to see each individual as unique and how we as a body of Christ need them all in order to strengthen, enhance and mature each of us to be more like him.

I have heard people talk about children in many different ways: as not ready to make a decision to follow Christ, or as having innate spiritual acuity; as those whom we should strive to be more like spiritually. Some lessen the spiritual lives of children. Some aggrandise them to the point of idealisation. I don't learn something new about myself and God from 'children'. I learn it from a person who happens to be a child.

When we listen to a sermon, we choose to say in our hearts, 'God is going to speak through you, and I am going to learn what I can, and I hope to change a little more into the person God is calling me to be.' We follow worship leaders where they lead us, giving them the benefit of the doubt if a song or two isn't right up our alley. We listen to each other when we give advice because we know that we don't know everything and that wisdom often comes through listening to each other. We do all of this not because preachers, pastors, worship leaders and small group leaders are adults. We do this because they are individuals made in God's image, specially gifted for their purpose in life, and used by God to impact, challenge, teach and encourage.

What would happen if I looked at all individuals as equal members of the body of Christ, regardless of age or faith experience? As members whom I need and who need me? What if our boxes of 'children', 'teens', 'adults' or 'new Christians' are robbing us of experiencing the blessing and power of the full body of Christ? Am I humble enough to look at a three-year-old girl, a twelve-year-old boy, or a 40-year-old who just responded to Christ last week and think, 'You are a creation of the living God, unique and powerful, with a purpose and a call on your life today and tomorrow. I want to learn from you and rejoice with you as we journey together in this life, transforming ourselves, our communities, and the nations'?

I do believe that the church in general has stood back from our children and said, 'We love you, we value you, but we don't need you.' But I don't think the way to correct that mistake is to say, 'OK, children and teens, now we need you.' I think the way to correct it is to say, 'OK. We see each one of you as an individual called by God. How can we empower each one of you individually to live your purpose in the body of Christ?'

Mentoring more than programme

Whenever we start opening our doors to individuals to serve in our churches and communities, we can rightly begin to be concerned about how to support this wide range of people. Our knee-jerk reaction can be to create a formal programme, but I don't believe that it is always necessary. I would encourage you to pair up these new volunteers with mentors who are willing to train and equip them in the practicalities of serving, and support them as they serve. This releases the stress of centralising a programme, while still allowing for the vulnerability and lack of experience of younger people and new members. There are some helpful points that I have found in doing this. Check out Appendix B at the back of this book to see a few models. Appendix A suggests a process for how to discuss these concepts with your church leadership and how to implement them within teams.

Value ministry from every person

Train your congregations to receive and value ministry from every person, from both adults and children. I have come across several churches who have wanted to create a more intergenerational feel to their church, but when they make moves to raise the children up, it doesn't work out in the way they hoped. It is important to expect that this is going to be a slow and gradual culture change. We aren't just saying, 'Let the children do more.' We are saying, 'Let's think about church differently.' That takes more than just changing the way we do church; it takes all of us going on a journey together: teaching children how to see themselves differently in a congregation, and teaching adults to be willing to explore a different feel to church.

There are different implementation models that you can see in the Appendices, but here I'd like to discuss how to help shift the perceptions of church and children in the minds of the adults.

In most churches, we communicate that we love our children and are glad that they are there. But do we model the expectation that children can contribute spiritually to the life of the church? You see, we often accept that children can contribute in token ways, but almost never in spiritual ones. We reinforce this by creating only opportunities for children in the church service that display them as 'cute'. We let them do a nativity play or sing a song. We invite them to share what they are learning in their children's groups, allowing them a chance to summarise an adult's teaching just to let them feel as if they were a part of the whole (but are not really). We let them read the Bible in the service, but rather than taking them seriously as readers, we applaud their performance when they finish.

Congregations have almost never experienced children as actual spiritual contributors to the whole. They don't know what it looks like. It takes a shift of expectation and some training for them to begin to see children as part of the functioning body of Christ.

So how can we begin to shift this?

Create opportunities

Create easy opportunities for congregation members of all ages and faith levels to contribute to the service. For example, have the first song of worship chosen by a congregation member. Before the start of worship, have that congregation member get up and explain why that song means so much to him, what his favourite line of the song is and why. People of all ages and all faith experiences can participate in this. It allows personal testimony of an individual's encounter with God, and it invites the congregation into a deeper experience of worship. You will be surprised which songs children love, and why. The first time I did this with our congregation, a five-year-old boy wanted to sing 'Amazing Grace' because they sang it at his grandad's funeral to remind them that one day they will all get to worship God together again. When asked what his favourite line was, he told the story of how he once got lost in a shop, and he was so scared that he started crying. He asked God to send someone to find him, and just then his mum rounded the corner and called out to him. He said his heart felt like it would fly out of his body with happiness. That's why his favourite line is, 'I once was lost, but now I'm found'. He figured that sometimes people feel lost from God and would be super-happy to be found by him just as he was found by his mum. I have never heard a congregation sing 'Amazing Grace' with such vigour after that, and there were tears in many people's eyes.

Model the attitude

Model from the front the attitude you are looking for and frame it for the congregation. When a child participates in the spiritual aspects of the service, don't praise their performance or have them applauded. The most positive feedback a child can receive is a genuine response to what they are trying to accomplish. People serve in the church to bless the congregation and to contribute to others' spiritual and personal experiences of God. We must allow children the dignity of doing that.

In the above example, the child was sharing about his favourite worship song. Instead of getting up afterwards and saying, 'Let's give Johnny a clap, well done,' say, 'Thank you for sharing that, Johnny. Singing "Amazing Grace" was a deeper experience for me personally because you shared that. I could picture myself in the future standing with the people I have loved who are already in heaven singing praise to God.'

Equip

Equip children and adults with the skills to respond. Whenever children are going to do something from the front, it will be a new experience for your congregation (be it sharing from their experience, or reading the Bible, or leading worship), and it is helpful to inform people how to approach the experience. If a child is sharing from the Bible, even a five-minute reflection on a verse, preface it for your congregation: 'We are all on a journey with God, and the strength of being part of a church is that we all get to learn from each other's experiences and lives. I was chatting with Enyo the other day, and she had some interesting insights into scripture, so I asked her to share with all of us. Let's position our hearts to receive from the word.' This is so much better than, 'Enyo wanted to come up here, so I said "Sure!" Enyo is the precious daughter of Tom and Susie, and we love them, and

I couldn't resist those pleading eyes. We are in for a treat! Come on up, Enyo!'

Provide scenarios

Provide scenarios for safe 'first times', setting up the individuals to 'succeed'. Not all opportunities will be within the service. There are serving opportunities all over church: welcome teams, PA teams, coffee teams, children's work teams, flower arranging, set-up, church magazines, toddler groups and lunches for the elderly. When we set children up in mentorship with an adult who will equip them and ensure they are supported, then we can ensure every opportunity can be a safe place to try it out. From crèche rotas to the welcome team, as long as each mentor knows how to empower a child's spiritual or physical contribution and help others to engage with that child, then the process of integration can go as slowly or as quickly as you wish.

*

— Chapter 11 —

FAQs

I'm a bit concerned that all of this 'love' stuff is going to make my child unwise about strangers. I don't want her just approaching random people on the street, or trusting casual acquaintances she meets at church. How do I keep my child safe while still teaching her how to love others?

Keeping our children safe is of utmost importance, and we need to be clear about this with our children as we disciple them. This is why 'establishing boundaries' is an important part of the six-stage circle. Here are a few thoughts about how to describe this to children:

- We always need to love wisely. Sometimes hurt people don't know how to receive love well or how to give it back safely. That's why it's important that we chat with our parents about how to love people safely and wisely.
- If you see an adult that you don't know who might need help, then go and chat to your parents or a safe adult whom you know well if your parents aren't around. Then you can decide together how to help.
- God is constantly talking to us, and if you ever feel uncomfortable around someone or in a situation, then that could be God's encouraging you to go and find someone you know to be safe around. It is not rude or unloving to take care of yourself and leave when you feel uncomfortable.
- Because we are powerful people, we are in charge of how we show our love. No one gets to demand love from us, or try to make us feel bad or as if we 'should' do something for them.

You will know your children's sensitivities and how to keep them safe. Establishing boundaries is an important life skill in living a life of love. As children grow, you can lay those foundations of how to help people who are hurting, as well as how to have healthy friendships, relationships and marriages.

What about the gifts of the Spirit? The supernatural ones like tongues and healing? Shouldn't we equip our children to learn how to use these?

I think that those of us within the charismatic church often so much desire that our children have all that the adults have, in terms of the things of the Spirit, that we can skew the emphasis too much on the performance of the gifts of the Spirit, instead of on the purpose of the gifts: for building up and encouraging others. We can become very focused on seeing these gifts in our children instead of cultivating their characters to be desperate to see God's love poured out on people. We should pray for healing when we are moved out of compassion and from a desire to see people reconnect with God and experience his love, not because we want to see a miracle. We should speak words of knowledge to bring freedom and release to someone, not to impress others by how godly we are or to see how accurate we can be. Love is the purpose of these gifts. As Paul wrote in his letter to the Christians of Corinth:

'If I speak in the tongues of men or of angels, but do not have love, I am only a resounding gong or a clanging cymbal. If I have the gift of prophecy and can fathom all mysteries and all knowledge, and if I have a faith that can move mountains, but do not have love, I am nothing. If I give all I possess to the poor and give over my body to hardship that I may boast, but do not have love, I gain nothing.' (1 Corinthians 13:1–4)

The process of discipling children in using these gifts is the same as training them how to use the gifts of mercy, faith or administration.

They are all gifts of the Spirit—supernatural gifts. We train them to love. We equip them to understand their purpose. We cultivate their character so that when they use the power of God they are humble and not proud. We practically equip them with skills to use the gifts well. This goes for all gifts, from discerning between spirits to giving. When you teach adults about these things, you tend to take it around the six-stage circle. I would encourage you to do the same with children.

So do I equip children to use all the gifts of the Spirit? Yes, I do. If you would like to know more about how to talk to your children about these gifts, how to equip them practically to use them, and what that looks like in the life of a child, head to www.rachelturner. org.uk.

Children and teens aren't as mature as adults. They are still young in their faith and could have wrong theologies. Don't we need to guard our pulpits? Doesn't our responsibility to the health and feeding of the congregation come before letting a child preach?

I believe that we are all on a journey of faith, and that children can share their reflections on scripture just as much as adults can. Like anyone who is new to preaching or new in the faith, they will need support to learn how to share those reflections with the wider congregation. I encourage every child who is looking to serve in any capacity to be matched up with someone who is willing to encourage and support that child in the skills needed to achieve it. I don't believe that what we are looking for from a child is a three-point, 45-minute hermeneutical analysis! What we are looking for is a person's sincere response to a portion of scripture, and a humble sharing of their insight as a snapshot of where they are with God and what they are learning. I believe that this is just as valid and has as much spiritual impact as the more intellectual sermon formats. When we allow children to preach, we also get to hear their wonderful perspectives. I remember hearing a child speak on Jeremiah 33:3: 'Call to me and I will answer you, and tell you great and unsearchable things you do not know.' Her main thought was, 'God is better than Google.' It was a unique, intriguing and simple sharing of how we think that we can find answers to pretty much anything in the world, but that we must not forget that there is only one person who can promise to give answers to things that are unsearchable. I don't know how many times that analogy has returned to me over the past year in my everyday life. It was probably the most memorable sermon of the year for me.

Children and teens can be really unreliable. We need people we can count on for our rotas at church. Won't letting children and teens serve cause havoc with our church efficiency?

There are three factors here:

- Choosing the right children: as with any volunteer, you should look at their character before you entrust them with critical responsibilities. New volunteers need to be trained before they are released, and often you will pick up on any character issue that needs to be quietly and respectfully addressed with them.
- Getting parents committed: in my experience, if a child fails to show up for their rota day, it is 70 per cent the parent's fault. They may schedule a family trip, holiday or something else on the child's day with little or no warning. I ask parents to sign a commitment form, stating that they recognise that their child is a powerful part of our community and that they support and encourage their child's commitment to be part of a team. Once parents are on board, most problems are solved.
- Holding individuals to account: as with any volunteer, teens and children need to be held accountable. Part of this is that it is essential to grow children and teens to the level of being

significantly responsible. It's no good making them a 'leader' if actually they are trusted with nothing. Trusting means accepting the real possibility of failure as part of their growth journey. If the teen doesn't show up, will it cause hardship, or are they actually just an added extra? No one likes being an added extra. It means that they don't count and aren't necessary. People need to be needed and appreciated. If they let you down by not showing up or by not doing the work, it is important for you to ask them what is going on, just as you would with an adult. Communicate the consequences for you and the church when they don't fulfil their responsibilities, and help process with them what happened and why you were let down.

What about having children on the prayer ministry team? Often people come up with serious issues that can be inappropriate for children. It could make the adult feel uncomfortable as well as the child. Wouldn't it be better if they didn't serve on the prayer ministry team?

These are valid concerns to raise, but it's important to try to solve the problem before banning children from that area of service. I think that there are two issues here: 1) a person coming forward for prayer and that subject being inappropriate for a child to hear. 2) a person feeling uncomfortable being prayed for by a child.

The fear that can arise in leaders is that we may be putting children in inappropriate situations while also putting people off receiving prayer. However, there are ways around both of these concerns. For example, if your church has prayer teams that work in pairs, have several prayer pairs that are adult only and some that are mixed teen/adult or child/adult. That way people can self-select which team they come to for prayer, allowing those who would feel uncomfortable to be able to choose differently without causing a disturbance. It is rare that someone with an inappropriate topic would come to a child/adult or teen/adult pairing, but if they do, then you can very quickly give the child a pre-arranged sign to go and join another team while you deal with this one on your own.

I think I should also highlight what would be considered 'inappropriate'. I would suggest you ask the child's parent what boundaries they would like for you to have for their child in this area. Personally, there are very few situations that I would feel would be inappropriate for a child or teen. I do not consider a crying adult to be 'inappropriate', for instance, but one whose behaviour may come across as scary would be. Topics that may be inappropriate I would encourage you to work out with the parents. Shielding a child isn't always the best thing for them. Children know that bad stuff happens in the world; it is not a surprise. When they are on the prayer ministry team, they can be a part of the solution, and see close up how God meets and ministers to the broken-hearted. If we shield them too much, they will miss out on the significant and powerful works of God in the face of difficulty.

There is a girl who wants to serve on the sound desk, but we have only men on the team. Should we find her a woman mentor?

My view would be that there is no need. We aren't looking for someone to be the child or teen's permanent life coach; we are looking for an existing team member to train, encourage and support a younger team member in service. I don't believe it matters whether it is a man or a woman. I have a high value for freedom in cross-gender pairings in service. I believe that in order for children and teens to have a healthy and positive view of themselves, it is helpful for them to be exposed to a variety of mentors and community members who love and invest in them. I believe that boys need to have the presence of godly men and godly women in their lives, and I believe that girls need to have the presence of godly men and godly women in their lives.

For me, the main issue isn't gender, but accountability. All mentoring should conform to accepted child protection guidelines, which means that mentors need to be DBS checked, with serving happening in public within a community. We are all members of the body with the same Spirit. I believe that we do ourselves and our children a disservice when we isolate them from learning from those of a different gender. I feel that too often churches trust in the gender divide to keep things 'safe' and are lax on accountability. I would rather create a culture of transparency, openness and accountability and enable all the members of the body to encourage and support all members, not just male to male, or female to female. How degrading and limiting is it to tell a 15-year-old girl that in order for her to serve her passion, she has to find a female who is inexperienced to teach her and be around for her safety! How disrespectful to that man who is willing to get involved!

This sounds easy for the 'serving' areas like welcoming and set-up, but there are children wanting to be involved in some of the up-front service ministries: preaching, leading prayers, and worship. What do we do?

Some children are called to more 'up-front' ministries. I'm sure you can ask your vicar or pastor when they first wanted to lead or preach, and how they went about that as a child or young person. I would suggest that you facilitate this in the same way as you would with adults. If a child wants to lead worship, have her serve in the worship band. As you grow her and when you think she is ready, have her lead a song from the set, and ensure that she is keeping to your values for leading worship, not just to the songs. Invite her into your planning sessions to help her understand how and why you shape what you are doing. Harness her insights to make worship more engaging for children. If and when you think she is ready, have her lead a small set for a small group of people (team meeting, breakfast meeting, or similar) and coach her through the process. Build up to it, the same as with everything else... little steps to preaching could be testimony slots, children's sections, talks in small groups, and eventually sharing from the word during the main service.

To be in leadership at our church, you have to be mature in your faith. Do we just skip all the character requirements because they are children?

Absolutely not, but we require of them a level of maturity appropriate for their age. It is unrealistic and unfair to demand that an eight-year-old boy have the emotional and spiritual maturity of a 30-year-old woman before he is allowed to lead people in worship. We can say, however, that a worship leader must be pursuing God, have humility and willingness to learn, and a determination to work hard. We acknowledge that the child is eight, and so we can give him opportunity to lead worship at a level that he can handle well, in accordance with his maturity and skill. As children grow in spiritual maturity, so will their opportunities and scale of ministry, just the same as with adults. We have to accept that they are on their journey of faith, and that journey is as valid as an adult's.

*

Appendices

*

Appendix A: Sharing the vision with your leadership team and congregation

Releasing children into serving in all areas of the church and enabling a fuller range of the church family to serve in all areas of the church has great rewards. In order to facilitate this well, though, it can be helpful to church leadership teams to think through the process and implications of this move carefully. The goal is for this to be seen as a blessing and strengthening of the church community, not as a radical and unpopular move with little fruit and a lot of work! Here are some suggested steps to get the ball rolling with senior leadership.

Cast the vision to them and resource their thinking. Often church leaders are balancing many different values and visions while trying to lead their church, and before we try to convince them how it might work logistically, they need to own the idea for themselves. They need to be convinced that it is important and valuable and will add momentum to their vision for the church; that it is a journey worth taking. Each church leader will be different, and each leadership team functions in a different way. Have a think about the best way in for your church. Maybe it will be a meeting with the main pastor, or finding a champion on the staff team who will partner with you. Would you rather gather other children's leaders to the idea and then go to the senior leadership team as a children's work team? What works best in your context? Another way to influence your senior leadership is to resource the way they think. Are they book readers? Or MP3 people? If so, find a resource to challenge their thinking on the topic; give them this book or other books that would help. Let them know that you are passionate about it and are willing to put in the work to help make it happen.

Gather people together to help to work out the practicalities of implementation. Senior leadership often want to be able to picture it in their minds, so some questions that would be good to wrestle with together are:

- Preparing the congregation: how do we begin to shape the hearts and minds of our congregation to be hungry for this? Do we do a sermon series, or include it in our church weekend away? Have a series of testimonies on a Sunday? Or put on a course?
- Training and equipping team leaders: what equipping do we need to do with team leaders and mentors? Are they ready for this? Will they need convincing? What support do they need so that they can implement this programme with the values and lessons that we have learned?
- Getting parents on board: how do we include and support parents in this process?
- Communicating to the children: how do we want to tell them? Do we want a big launch day, or a one-on-one approach?
- Covering practicalities: who will need to be DBS checked and how do we do that? Are there any policies that we need to add anything to (prayer ministry, for example) to ensure that children are welcomed and protected? If we really consider these children and young people as full members of our team, does that mean that we should change the meetings to a time when they are able to come?
- Establishing boundaries: are there any areas of ministry that we feel should be closed to children or young people? Why is that, and is it a valid reason? Or do we just need to be creative in how to manage it?
- Launching the integration: how do we want to go about releasing the full body and then communicate and empower it well?
- Continuing assessment: how are we going to measure the fruit of this? How will we know if it's going well or poorly? What are the values we have for the full body, and how do we ensure that the mentors are mentoring with these values?

We can see this in action by looking at some options.

One church may come up with a model that says: 'Our church wants one big launch day, a flinging open of the doors in a demonstrative way.'

For two months, the senior leadership team, with key players from the children and youth team, plan the implementation of empowering children and young people to serve in all areas of the church. Team leaders are consulted and prep their teams, recruit mentors and create space on the rota for the following term, and a plan that everyone is happy with is ready to go. An optional training evening is run for mentors to answer their questions and equip them for their new role.

Launch day arrives. On one Sunday there is preaching in all services about the importance of every member of the church serving as part of the body of Christ, basing it in scripture and testimony and giving the whole congregation an opportunity to respond by signing up for teams. At the same time, the children's leaders cast the vision to the children and facilitate them to take the next step. Packs are given to the children that include a catalogue of possible serving areas, an application form for the children to fill out, and a commitment form for parents to sign saying that they will support their child's serving responsibilities.

The following week sign-ups begin. A central administrator/ organiser collects the forms from the children and passes them to the team leaders, who then call to chat to the parents and children, inviting them for a 'trial session' to observe and try out in the area where they would like to serve.

Following this, children and young people go on the rota alongside their mentors and are seen all over the congregation serving in all areas.

Two people have been assigned to do weekly follow-ups with mentors and children for a month, and then a three-month brief review is scheduled, as well as a six-month full review to assess what fruit is being seen and what needs to be adapted.

Another option would be the softly-softly approach; no launch day in sight for this church. They have decided that, as a staff team, they will read a book together about the body of Christ and spend two months wrestling with the ideas and asking and answering questions about the concept. A decision is made that a more organic approach would be best. Individual team leaders who already have a heart for children serving are approached about welcoming children to serve, and are envisioned and equipped one-on-one through informal conversations.

As the individual team leaders are ready and happy to have children serve in their teams, children's leaders begin to ask children about their interest in serving in those areas. If children are interested, the children's leaders chat with the parents and introduce the families to those team leaders after church. Team leaders work with those families to enable children to start serving with their mentors.

Throughout the year, more teams take on individual children, addressing concerns as they arise and opening up more and more areas of ministry.

After about nine months, children's leaders have conversations with team leaders, parents and children to see how it has been going and if it is producing the spiritual fruit in the children and in the congregation that was desired. Whatever the results, a four-week sermon series about the body of Christ is run. One Sunday covers the importance of each member serving, no matter what their age, pointing out the journey of the church in retrospect. This could highlight what has been occurring and have the testimonies of children, team leaders, congregation members and parents about how the move towards a fuller body has affected them.

*

Appendix B: Models for implementation

Small church (between one and 50 children)

In small churches, I suggest that first of all a passionate person who wants to facilitate the growing of children in ministry takes the lead and brings this vision to the senior leadership team. Appendix A can help that leadership team think through any adjustments that would need to be made to allow space for more people to minister.

The second stage is to chat to team leaders and find people who would be willing to mentor and grow younger individuals who want to serve in particular areas. Approach people you think would be great, as well as unexpected people or those who have turned you down in the past, about helping with children's or youth work. You may find that people who have no interest in delivering curriculum on a Sunday for a children's group are the best mentors ever for two 14-year-old boys who are passionate about audiovisuals. It is also important for team leaders to feel empowered to walk the line between wanting to welcome individuals on to their team, and being wise about who they recruit. It is OK for them to have in their heads what kind of team member they are looking for, and to set boundaries and think creatively about how to empower children to serve while not compromising the efficiency of the team. For instance, if a four-year-old girl is desperate to serve on the welcome team, but the team leader is hesitant because she doesn't have anyone to support the child in case she gets distracted, then you can suggest that until the team gets bigger, the girl brings a parent or family friend to support her.

The third stage is to talk to parents about the vision behind having their children serve in church, and to encourage them to chat to their children about where they feel God is asking them to serve in the church or community. This allows parents to be at the centre of this discussion, able to coach their children in it and to decide on boundaries before issues come up.

The fourth stage is to match up children and mentors. There are endless ways you could do this. In a small church, people tend to know the children and young people well, whether they are the parents, family friends or children's leaders. You may feel comfortable simply to ask the mentors to feel free to speak to the children, teens and parents directly when they spot a gift, skill or passion. If ten-year-old William is constantly playing with cables and hanging around the sound desk, and a mentor spots that, then the most natural thing is for that mentor to mention to William that if he ever wanted to serve on the team, the church could really use his skills and passions in that area, and encourage him to chat to his parents about it. The mentor can follow this up with William's parents, mentioning that he would be happy to have William with him on the rota and train him until he is skilled enough to take his own slot. If the parents are happy, William is happy and the mentor is happy, then William does the same thing that everyone else at the church does to join and serve on that team, and is held to the same standard that everyone else is.

Another approach is to have the children's leaders function as advocates. They can use their knowledge of the children to have conversations with them and the parents, and when a child knows what area he wants to serve in, the children's leader does the initial introduction to the mentor or team leader and helps to facilitate that connection. After that, the team leader or mentor can take over and the child or teen then does the same thing that everyone else at the church does to join and serve on that team, and is held to the same standard that everyone else is.

Large church (50 children or more)

The first thing you will need is a champion for the cause who is willing to take the lead, and a key person on the leadership team who can represent the vision at staff meetings and the like. They could be the same person, but they don't have to be. With a larger church, it is important that the ripple effects get pondered collectively and strategies are lined up well, so that everybody involved can find this process peaceful and life-giving, instead of surprising and disconcerting. Appendix A has some suggestions for issues that senior leadership teams often need to think through before implementation can move forward.

Secondly, it is important to involve team leaders in the idea development of this vision. Team leaders have vision and strategy, and it is important to get their buy-in, especially in large churches. Meet with them and share some of your heart about individuals serving where they are called, even children. Often team leaders may invite you to talk to their team during their termly team meeting to cast the vision and answer questions, or they may want to do that themselves and get mentors to sign up with them. As I mentioned in detail in the small church model, it is important to empower the team leaders to think through how to facilitate the children, as well as any guidelines they may have in selecting children as team members.

Thirdly, parents need to be consulted and brought on board with the vision. In a larger church, parents tend to be more concerned about the logistics than in a smaller, more organic church. It may help to run an information night about how the church wants to empower all of its members to serve in the church, and what that will look like. You could run a 'Parenting for Purpose' course in the lead-up to communication, so that parents are prepped and ready to coach their children in their participation. Have a parent commitment form as part of the children's sign-up process, so that as the children sign up to be a part of ministry, the parents sign a commitment to support their child in it.

Fourthly, the matching-up of children and mentors takes place. This can be done in many different ways. I have personally facilitated each child in connecting to the relevant team leader, who then assigned the child a mentor. I have also run the process by asking each child to fill out an application form, which included questions about the child's heart and calling, so that mentors could get to know the child a bit and choose whom they wanted to mentor. The consideration here is that the teams may be so large that you as a parent or children's leader may need to be more paperwork-based to ensure that the heart-to-heart is facilitated instead of descending into a logistics exercise.

Parenting Children for a Life of Faith

Helping children meet and know God

Nurturing children in the Christian faith is a privilege given to all of us whose prime job it is to raise children. God's desire is that our parenting should guide each child to meet and know him, and to live with him every day through to eternity.

Parenting Children for a Life of Faith explores how the home can become the primary place in which children are nurtured into the reality of God's presence and love, equipped to access him themselves and encouraged to grow in a two-way relationship with him that will last a lifetime.

The basic principle behind the ideas explored is that we need to model for our children what it means to be in a relationship with God rather than just equipping them to know about him—helping our children to be God-connected rather than just God-smart.

Each chapter includes encouraging true stories and questions to help us reflect on our own experience as we journey together with our children.

ISBN 978 1 84101 607 8   £7.99
Available from your local Christian bookshop or direct from BRF:
www.brfonline.org.uk.

Rachel Turner is also writing *Parenting Children for a Life of Identity: Releasing children to be who they were designed to be*, available from July 2015.

Family Fun for Summer

30 holiday activities for families to share

Jane Butcher

Crafts, food, games, word searches, treasure hunts…

Summer time, the longer days and school holidays offer more time for families to spend time together to talk, play and reconnect with one another in the midst of busy family life. *Family Fun for Summer* provides 30 'fun on a budget' activities to help you to spend quality time with your children over the summer, to explore faith in the home, and to have lots of fun together in the process!

Just what every family needs.
MICHELE GUINNESS

ISBN 978 0 85746 061 5   £4.99
Available from your local Christian bookshop or direct from BRF:
www.brfonline.org.uk.

Also available: *Family Fun for Christmas: 30 Advent and Christmas activities for families to share* and *Family Fun for Easter: 30 Lent and Easter activities for families to share*.

Side by Side with God in Everyday Life

Helping children to grow with God through all times

Yvonne Morris

Side by Side with God in Everyday Life invites churches and families alike to use a simple retelling of stories from the Bible as the basis for helping children to think more deeply about a wide range of everyday topics.

In total there are 28 easy-to-use story-based sessions, each one featuring one of the times and seasons outlined in Ecclesiastes 3:1–8, such as birth, death, planting, uprooting, laughing, mourning, dancing, giving, listening, love, hate, war and peace.

Each session picks out two related Bible stories, one to set the scene and the other to go deeper into the theme. These simple retellings can be used to promote open questions, reflection, discussion, further exploration and prayer, and readily act as prompts towards a deeper understanding of what it means to walk side by side with God in everything we do. Ideal for 6–10s.

ISBN 978 1 84101 855 3   £7.99

Available from your local Christian bookshop or direct from BRF:
www.brfonline.org.uk.

Enjoyed

this book?

Write a review—we'd love to hear what you think.
Email: reviews@brf.org.uk

Keep up to date—receive details of our new books as they happen.
Sign up for email news and select your interest groups at:
www.brfonline.org.uk/findoutmore/

Follow us on Twitter @brfonline

By post—to receive new title information by post (UK only), complete the form below and post to: BRF Mailing Lists, 15 The Chambers, Vineyard, Abingdon, Oxfordshire, OX14 3FE

Your Details
Name _____
Address_____
_____
Town/City _____ Post Code _____
Email_____

Your Interest Groups (*Please tick as appropriate)	
☐ Advent/Lent	☐ Messy Church
☐ Bible Reading & Study	☐ Pastoral
☐ Children's Books	☐ Prayer & Spirituality
☐ Discipleship	☐ Resources for Children's Church
☐ Leadership	☐ Resources for Schools

Support your local bookshop
Ask about their new title information schemes.